"One of the main thrusts of the Pauline Epistles is to reveal the divine nature of the Christ Jesus who had appeared to Paul on the Damascus road. The Epistle to the Church at Colossae is a prime example of this. Verse by verse he unveils facets of the nature of Christ Jesus that may easily have escaped us in the Gospels. Without ever once detracting from the humanity of Jesus, Paul masterfully attracts our attention to the divine nature of the Christ. He reveals Him as the source or fountainhead of every provision God has made for the saints in this world.

"This book examines only those provisions in Christ that Paul discusses in chapter one of Colossians, but even those should greatly expand our comprehension of our Lord Jesus Christ."

BY Judson Cornwall

Let Us Abide
Let Us Enjoy Forgiveness
Let Us See Jesus
Let Us Praise
Let Us Draw Near
Let Us Be Holy
Heaven

Let Us See Jesus
Judson Cornwall

Fleming H. Revell, Company
Old Tappan, New Jersey

Library of Congress Cataloging in Publication Data
Cornwall, E   Judson.
Let us see Jesus.

   1. Jesus Christ—Person and offices.   2. Bible.
N.T. Colossians—Criticism, interpretation, etc.
I. Title.
BT202.C685   232   80-20645
ISBN 0-8007-5052-7

To Eleanor Cornwall,
whose deep love for Jesus has made
her an even more devoted wife and mother

Contents

		Acknowledgments		9
		Preface		11
			Colossians 1	13
1	Jesus' Apostle	Verse One		15
2	Jesus, Source of Grace	Verse Two		21
3	Jesus, Source of Peace	Verse Two		32
4	Jesus, Object of Our Faith	Verse Four		43
5	Jesus, Source of Love	Verse Four		53
6	Jesus, Our Hope	Verse Five		61
7	Jesus, Our Deliverer	Verse Thirteen		74
8	Jesus, Our King	Verse Thirteen		92
9	Jesus, Our Redeemer	Verse Fourteen		103
10	Jesus, the Image of God	Verse Fifteen		116
11	Jesus, the Creator	Verse Seventeen		126
12	Jesus, the Head of the Church	Verse Eighteen		137
13	Jesus, the Reconcilor	Verse Twenty		148

Acknowledgments

It is not an idle statement when I affirm that without Vonnie McClure this book probably would never have been written. The first contract I ever signed for a book had this title, but, instead, I wrote on praise. Six other books and three minibooks followed, but this title remained far in the background. Still, I couldn't forget how blessed this series had been in conferences where I had preached it, and I had transcriptions of those tapes on file in my study.

In 1978, while I was ministering in her husband's church, Vonnie and I began to discuss the possibilities of this book. She urged me to get it written, and when I pleaded business and a commitment to another book contract, she offered to help in whatever way she could. Because of her years of editorial and writing experience, I agreed to let her do the first draft of those chapters that had been transcribed. Additionally, she edited my final drafts and typed them for me. It is my prayer that the long hours she has invested in this book will be a blessing to the body of Christ.

Preface

Our introduction to the divine usually begins with an introduction to the Jesus of the Gospels. We see the perfect God-man from His incarnate infancy to His ignominious impalement on the cross. We watch Him mature, enter His ministry, and train His associate ministers. We see Him hungry, thirsty, and weary. We observe Him being moved with compassion, love, and even anger. We see Him loved and hated, received and rejected, praised and perjured. Although His miracles attest to His divinity, we are overwhelmed by His majestic humanity. Because He is one of us as well as part of God we can relate to Him without being threatened.

But for too many Christians this concept of Jesus is never allowed to mature. They seldom see beyond His humanity into His divinity. He forever remains as Jesus: "my Saviour," "my healer," "my friend," or "my provider." He is visualized as their super "need meeter," but is seldom if ever seen as God.

Yet once we leave the Gospels we never read of "Jesus"; it is always "Christ Jesus," or "the Lord Jesus Christ," for from the day of His Resurrection the disciples saw Him as the *Lord* (John 20:20,-28), a word used as a substitute for the sacred name of God which the Jews considered too sacred to be pronounced aloud.

One of the main thrusts of the Pauline Epistles is to reveal the divine nature of the Christ Jesus who had appeared to Paul on the Damascus road. The Epistle to the Church at Colossae is a prime example of this. Verse by verse he unveils facets of the nature of Christ Jesus that may easily have escaped us in the Gospels. Without ever once detracting from the humanity of Jesus, Paul masterfully attracts our attention to the divine nature of the Christ. He reveals Him as the source or fountainhead of every provision God has made for the saints in this world.

This book examines only those provisions in Christ that Paul discusses in chapter one of Colossians, but even those should greatly expand our comprehension of our Lord Jesus Christ.

The choice of thirteen chapters for this book was very deliberate, for Jesus, who was the fourth man in the fire in Daniel's day, was the thirteenth man throughout the Gospels. It was always "Jesus and the twelve." So important did this number seem to be that after Judas committed suicide the remaining eleven elected a replacement for him so that they could maintain the number twelve, and later Christ Jesus added His own apostle, Paul, again bringing the number back to thirteen. So it seemed fitting to have thirteen, not twelve or fourteen, chapters.

COLOSSIANS

CHAPTER 1

PAUL, an apostle of Jesus Christ by the will of God, and Tĭmŏth-ĕ-ŭs *our* brother,

2 To the saints and faithful brethren in Christ which are at Cŏ-lŏs´-sē: Grace *be* unto you, and peace, from God our Father and the Lord Jesus Christ.

3 We give thanks to God and the Father of our Lord Jesus Christ, praying always for you,

4 Since we heard of your faith in Christ Jesus, and of the love *which ye have* to all the saints,

5 For the hope which is laid up for you in heaven, whereof ye heard before in the word of the truth of the gospel,

6 Which is come unto you, as *it is* in all the world; and bringeth forth fruit, as *it doth* also in you, since the day ye heard *of it*, and knew the grace of God in truth:

7 As ye also learned of Ĕp´-ă-phrăs our dear fellow-servant, who is for you a faithful minister of Christ;

8 Who also declared unto us your love in the Spirit.

9 For this cause we also, since the day we heard *it*, do not cease to pray for you, and to desire that *ye* might be filled with the knowledge of his will in all wisdon and spiritual understanding;

10 That ye might walk worthy of the Lord unto all pleasing, being fruitful in every good work, and increasing in the knowledge of God;

11 Strengthened with all might, according to his glorious power, unto all patience and longsuffering with joyfulness;

12 Giving thanks unto the Father, which hath made us meet to be partakers of the inheritance of the saints in light:

13 Who hath delivered us from the power of darkness, and hath translated *us* into the kingdom of his dear Son:

14 In whom we have redemption through his blood, *even* the forgiveness of sins:

15 Who is the image of the invisible God, the firstborn of every creature:

16 For by him were all things created, that are in heaven, and that are in earth, visible and invisible, whether *they be* thrones, or dominions, or principalities, or powers; all things were created by him, and for him:

17 And he is before all things, and by him all things consist.

18 And he is the head of the body, the church: who is the beginning, the firstborn from the dead; that in all *things* he might have the preeminence.

19 For it pleased *the Father* that in him should all fulness dwell;

20 And, having made peace through the blood of his cross, by him to reconcile all things unto himself; by him, *I say*, whether *they be* things in earth, or things in heaven.

21 And you, that were something alienated and enemies in *your* mind by wicked works, yet now hath he reconciled

22 In the body of his flesh through death, to present you holy and unblameable and unreproveable in his sight:

1

Jesus' Apostle

"Paul, an apostle of Jesus Christ by the will of God, and Timotheus our brother" (Colossians 1:1).

From the day the angel of the Lord told Joseph, ". . . thou shalt call his name JESUS: for he shall save his people from their sins" (Matthew 1:21), mankind has been unable to ignore this Jesus. His disciples were so overawed by the human Jesus as to leave their businesses and follow Him at His simple command, "Follow me" (Matthew 4:19). The Greeks urged Philip to intercede with Jesus to get them an appointment with Him (John 12:21), and the multitudes thronged Him wherever He went. His adversaries dogged His trail seeking an occasion against Him, while His admirers doted on every word He spoke. Some proclaimed Him as a king, but the religious rulers declared Him an imposter, while the believers seemed confused as to whether He was a prophet or their Messiah.

Although attitudes toward Jesus varied greatly, He was not to be ignored. Indeed, He couldn't be ignored. His presence could stir an entire city, for He broke up funeral processions by restoring the dead persons back to life; He healed the sick, opened blinded eyes, and lovingly touched lepers throughout the whole of Israel. He had to be reckoned with, for His gentle Spirit only camouflaged His revolutionary ways. He championed rights of women in a day when they were mere vassal slaves of their husbands, and yet He taught submission to the Roman oppressors when He knew that revolution stirred in the breast of every Israelite male.

To say that He was unpredictable would be an understatement, for everyone who sought to outguess Him, outmaneuver Him, or trick Him into a contradiction, always came out the losers. Even His enemies had to testify, "Never man spake like this man . . ." (John 7:46). When He was urged to share in judgment against a woman taken in adultery, Jesus shamed her accusers into leaving the scene, and then He freely forgave the woman, but later He scathingly rebuked the leading religious party, calling them hypocrites. Jesus exonerated sinners but exposed religionists.

Is it any wonder that men held greatly contrasting opinions about Jesus? Actually this dichotomy of attitude toward Jesus has continued long after His Resurrection from the dead and His Ascension to the Father. Although fiercely hated by some and passionately loved by others, Jesus has, nonetheless, affected the lives of all living persons on the face of the earth, whether they know it or not.

Countless martyrs sacrificed their lives because of their faith in Jesus, while other thousands were killed in religious inquisitions and so-called holy wars. Yet the very governments that sought to stamp out Christianity succeeded only in making Jesus all the more known throughout their kingdoms, for the blood of the martyrs has always been the seed of the Church.

Nevertheless, He has not only been the cause of the early deaths of His followers but He also has become the very source of each life and the object of that life's expression. More songs have been written and sung about Jesus than anyone else in all of history. Furthermore, millions of books have been written about Him, and His Book, the Bible, has been translated and printed in more languages and dialects than any other book. His message is proclaimed worldwide by missionaries, ministers, printed literature, radio and television broadcasts, and personal testimony.

He is so loved, revered, and cherished that buildings in His honor dot the landscape of the world. Who could estimate the multiple billions of dollars that have been spent throughout the world in erecting churches, synagogues, temples, and cathedrals in His honor and unto His worship? Or who could visualize how vast the number of men and women who have dedicated their lives to His service?

Actually, the name of Jesus is on the lips of nearly every American. His enemies use His name in profanity, while His adherents use it as a prayer. He is blessed and blasphemed; cherished and cursed; criticized and commended; but He is in our consciousness and very much a part of our language. His short sojourn in this world so changed the course of mankind that all have been affected in one way or the other, even in our speech patterns.

It is this Jesus who arrested Paul on his Damascus mission to destroy the Church. The blinding light of Christ's presence so sapped Paul's strength that he fell to the ground, fully aware of a voice speaking to him. "Who art thou, Lord?" Paul asked. "I am Jesus whom thou persecutest ..." was the answer (Acts 9:5). But for Paul, that answer was insufficient, and he spent the rest of his life seeking to know who this Jesus really was. Although Paul did not have an association with Jesus in the flesh, he came to know Him through divine revelation in such a way that when he wrote about the events of the last passover feast that Jesus had with His disciples, we might suppose that he had witnessed it in person, for he said, "I have received of the Lord that which also I delivered unto you ..." (1 Corinthians 11:23).

Later in his life, after years of missionary ministry and preaching, teaching, and writing to the churches, Paul cried, *"That I may know him,* and the power of his resurrection, and the fellowship of his sufferings, being made conformable unto his death" (Philippians 3:10, italics added). Paul's quest was still not over.

Although Paul obviously spent time in questioning the disciples and believers who had known Jesus during the years of His earthly pilgrimage, the things he reveals about Jesus in his Epistles were not gleaned from the Gospel writers; they came through divine revelation, for Paul speaks of Jesus as exalted, glorified, deified, and almighty. He places Christ on the throne in heaven, not on the cross of Calvary, and calls Him "the head of the body, the church ..." (Colossians 1:18), and "the Son of God with power ..." (Romans 1:4). Paul specialized in Jesus. Christ Jesus became the theme of Paul's writing, the lyric of his song, and the object of his praises. Paul was content with any lot in life if it included the presence of Jesus. He was the Lord's apostle, and he was happy about it.

When Paul wrote to the saints in Colossae, he used the same introductory statement he had used six other times: "Paul, an apostle of Jesus Christ . . ." (Colossians 1:1). We more frequently refer to him as being an apostle to the Church, or the apostle of the Gentiles, but Paul preferred to consider himself "an apostle of Jesus Christ."

The Greek word translated here as "apostle" is *apostolos,* which has at least four shades of meaning: a delegate, an ambassador, a commissioner, and a messenger. Paul felt that he was all these things for and with Jesus Christ.

As a *delegate* of Jesus, Paul functioned with divinely conferred authority. Nothing he said or did issued from personal desire or ambition; he functioned in delegated authority. He did not cast out demons in his name, but in the name of Jesus. He healed the sick and preached the Gospel amidst mighty signs and wonders, all in an authority and ability that had been delegated to him by Christ Jesus.

He considered himself a delegate acting in Christ's behalf, casting a proxy vote when it was needed. To the Church at Corinth he said, ". . . we pray you *in Christ's stead . . .*" (2 Corinthians 5:20, italics added). Paul never felt that the Ascension of Jesus caused His work to cease here on the earth; it merely required someone else to do that task with delegated authority. Paul accepted the appointment to be that delegate in his generation.

As an *ambassador,* Paul represented Christ Jesus in the governmental affairs of heaven on this earth. Paul sensed that an answer to Christ's prayer, ". . . Thy will be done in earth, as it is in heaven" (Matthew 6:10), required an ambassador here on earth to represent constantly heaven's will on earth, and he accepted that appointment (2 Corinthians 5:20; Ephesians 6:20).

As Christ's personal representative here on the earth, Paul withstood the Jewish high priest, vacillating Peter, and his persecuting brethren. He brought the testimony of Jesus into the synagogues of

the Greco-Roman world, and stepped from dungeon cells to represent Christ before kings. Whether they were Jews or Gentiles, com-
moners or kings, Paul always approached them as an ambassador
of the heavenly kingdom of Jesus Christ. Paul did not represent the
Jewish church in Jerusalem or the Gentile church in Antioch; he
represented Christ Jesus from heaven everywhere and at all times.
He was an apostolic ambassador of Jesus, and he considered every
place he went a heavenly embassy. He could make a jail cell function as a judicial hall.

As an apostle of Jesus, Paul was also a *commissioner* of Jesus'
functioning *with* Christ. Paul was involved in the divine government as a department head fully aware of specific responsibilities
and duties that came with the position. He did not parade, he performed; he did not seek to be served, he became the servant. He
did not demand a salary, instead he often supported himself as a
tentmaker; nor did he seem to expect divine vindication of his actions, for he accepted imprisonment as coming more from the
hand of God than the hands of men. But whatever he did, and
wherever he found himself, Paul possessed a keen sense of together-
ness with Jesus. He was doing or going *with* Him. He was serving in
the heavenly government *with* King Jesus. Paul was conscientious
and comfortable in his apostolic role as a commissioner in the spiritual government of Jesus Christ.

As a *messenger,* Paul was unexcelled. He developed a spiritual
sensitivity that enabled him to hear Christ's voice plainly and accurately. He did not hesitate declaring that his message came from
the Lord, and if he communicated anything out of his own experience levels he honorably said, "But to the rest speak I, not the Lord
. . ." (1 Corinthians 7:12).

As an apostolic messenger Paul not only heard accurately but
also communicated that message in written form so that undisci-
plined memories would not dilute or pollute it, and so that men he
would never meet could receive it.

Paul not only had a message; he both lived that message and
lived worthy of being a messenger of Jesus Christ. He disciplined
himself to such a level of obedience to the message that he communicated as much by the example of his life as he did by the ex-

pression of his lips. He could comfortably tell the saints in Thessalonica, ". . . ye ought to follow us: for we behaved not ourselves disorderly among you" (2 Thessalonians 3:7). Because of this, Paul accurately communicated both the words which he had heard and the nature of the One who had spoken them. He shared the divine message in divine faith and love.

Paul was also concerned about the reception of the message. Where the message was received in unbelief he reinforced the communication with supernatural demonstration. He did not leave it to the hearer to determine whether or not the message came from Jesus; he proved its divine authenticity with divine action. He attested, "For our gospel came not unto you in word only, but also in power, and in the Holy Ghost, and in much assurance . . ." (1 Thessalonians 1:5). He was a messenger of Jesus, and he would not have either the message or the sender of that message ignored.

It is this Paul, this apostle of Jesus Christ, who presents such a many-faceted image of Jesus in the opening statements of his letter to the saints at Colossae. This delegate of Jesus; this ambassador of Christ; this commissioner of God's Son; this messenger of the Lord, knew Jesus as the source of our needs, the object of our responses, and the total fulfillment of God's purposes. Is anyone, then, more qualified than he to introduce us to this Jesus?

Without setting aside preconceived notions about our wonderful Jesus, join the master expositor Paul as he paints many-hued word pictures of God's only Son, our Lord and Saviour Jesus Christ. Let us see Jesus as He is.

2

Jesus, Source of Grace

"To the saints and faithful brethren in Christ which are at Colosse: Grace be unto you. . . " (Colossians 1:2).

Receiving a letter from a beloved friend can be an exciting moment in any day. The flow of words on the page becomes communication that produces a communing between the two of you. Surely it was no less so when the Church at Colossae received Paul's letter. I wonder if in their excitement they ignored the letterhead and salutation and rushed into the body of the letter as we are so prone to do.

But much can be learned from the letterhead, for it establishes who the writer is, something of the company he represents, and it often gives the position the writer holds in that firm. Paul's letterhead is no exception. It reads, "Paul, an apostle of Jesus Christ by the will of God . . ." (Colossians 1:1). The message was coming from the firm of God the Father and God the Son, and the writer's position in that firm was "apostle." That he was not a self-appointed apostle is made clear in his statement ". . . by the will of God," and the inclusion of ". . . and Timotheus our brother" indicates that Paul did not set himself above or apart from the brethren. As a matter of record, Paul always took at least one other person with him on his ministry journeys.

Not only do we habitually ignore the letterhead upon which the letter is written but we also usually gloss over the salutation with which the letter begins. Recently there has been an attempt to discontinue the use of salutations in letters, especially in business correspondence, because it is claimed that it serves no useful purpose, is rarely read, and is, therefore, a waste of secretarial energy. To reinforce their point, several of these proponents wrote multiple letters to business firms with senseless salutations such as "Deer Antler," "Honorless One," "To Whom It Is of No Concern," and so on, and it was never called to their attention.

"No one reads a salutation anymore," they contended.

Perhaps they are right, for I read the book of Colossians repeatedly before I actually took time to read its salutations.

Dear Sir:

"To the saints and faithful brethren in Christ which are at Colosse . . ." Paul uses for his addressees. It may well have been fitting for Paul to use the double description of these Colossian Christians, for even today it often seems that many saints are not too faithful while the faithful in the Church aren't very saintly. It is possible Paul was addressing two separate groups of people in the Church.

Having established both who is writing this letter and to whom it was being written, Paul writes his standard salutation: "Grace be unto you, and peace. . . ." All of Paul's letters begin this way except 2 Timothy and Titus, where it is expanded to add the blessing of "mercy" to the grace and peace. Was Paul merely caught in the grip of a habit, or was grace the uppermost message in his mind when he ministered to a body of believers?

Man has built many doctrines around the message of the grace of God, and entire denominations have arisen to perpetuate and promulgate these doctrines. But sadly enough, these doctrines have often divided the body of Christ far more than they have blessed it. It is possible to get so enmeshed in a doctrine that we fail to see the One from whom this doctrinal truth has proceeded. The fundamental purpose of doctrine is to help us better understand Jesus, from whom the truth has come, but too frequently we divide ourselves and break Christian fellowship instead of coming to the source of truth that we might be united in Christ Jesus the Lord. Anything less than this will tend to death, not life. We settle for creed and concept rather than reaching for Christ's commitment to us. Grace is receivable or else Paul would not have given it to the saints.

What Grace Is *Not*

Grace is not merely a doctrine. Although the Church has a variety of concepts of grace and has developed diverse doctrines around this subject, no man ever found grace by merely embracing a doctrinal creed. No change in our concept can affect our standing before God. It is far less what my mouth says and far more what God's Word declares that makes grace receivable. The doctrine cannot impart grace; it merely attempts to interpret it. It is not the source; it is the sequel.

Grace is not a church name, even though there are scattered churches in America that choose to use the word *grace* in their title. The word in the name neither produces the grace nor assures anyone that God's grace is available in that location any more than the inclusion of the word *friendly* in a church name assures a visitor a friendly reception.

Grace is not a mental outlook. It is sometimes purported that the preaching of grace equals a declaration of positive thinking; but while grace will make us positive, being positive, however helpful it may be, is not synonymous with grace. I have watched people try to change their minds about behavior and guilt, declaring their new mental attitude "grace," and have had to minister to them after they had a breakdown. They had not come into the flow and life of grace; they had merely sought to exchange one set of laws for another, but they were still under law, not grace.

Grace is not an excuse for disobedience. Too frequently we meet the excuse, "I know what the Word of God says, but, thank God, I'm under grace, not under the law."

Being in or under grace never allows us to be disobedient to the Word of God, for it is inviolate, and we have no right to call the Bible "law" and the Spirit "grace," for the Spirit and the Word always agree inasmuch as one is the author and the second is what was written.

Grace is not a product of the law. Galatians 3:23 says, "But before faith came, we were kept under the law, shut up . . . ." The original Greek word here translated as "shut up" is a military term that would more properly be translated "stockaded." The law was God's stockade or prison that kept us from self-destruction until faith was revealed to us. The product of a prison is not freedom, for these terms are actually antithesis to each other, hence saying that grace is the end result of the law is incongruous. This portion of Galatians shows that we move from law to faith, not from law to grace, for law was God's protective custody until faith came. When the believer moves into a life of faith he is released from the stockade of law and exposed to divine grace.

Grace is not disgrace. Some Christians exercise behavior patterns under the banner of "grace" that are a total disgrace to the Church of the Lord Jesus Christ. They seem to function under the misconception that "grace" is an automatic covering for a believer's sins, inconsistencies, and errors; that it is like a savings account coupled to a checking account in an automatic transfer to cover any overdraft. But this is neither the nature nor function of God's grace.

Grace is not permissiveness; it is persuasion.

Grace is not license; it is liberty!

When the Apostle Paul offered grace to the churches he presented something far greater than doctrine or creed; far higher than a title or name; far more majestic than a mental outlook; and far more dignified than an absolution for disobedience to the Word of God. He prayed that a divine energy might flow from the heart of Christ Jesus into the lives of the believers who form His body here on this earth, and he expected his prayer to be answered.

What Grace *Is*

Knowing what grace is not does not, in itself, define what grace actually is; it merely limits our search somewhat. A very old and often quoted definition of grace is, "the unmerited favor of God." Essentially this is true, but it is far too limited a definition, for absolutely every good we receive from God is unmerited. By this definition anything short of hell would be classified as grace.

The subject of grace expands consistently throughout the pages of the New Testament. In John's prologue to the fourth Gospel he introduces us to the *Logos,* the Word of God, who was made flesh in the person of the Lord Jesus Christ. He states that He "dwelt among us (and we beheld His glory...) full of *grace* and *truth*" (John 1:14, italics added). This is the same combination that Paul uses here in Colossians 1:6 where he writes, "... the grace of God in truth."

It is certainly no accident that these two apostles connect grace and truth, for they are inseparable qualities of the Lord Himself. Grace and truth must flow together to be life-giving as surely as hydrogen and oxygen must combine to produce life-giving water. Separated they are explosive combustibles, dangerous to handle. Grace apart from truth is dangerous, while truth minus grace can be very destructive. When the grace of forgiveness is embraced without the truth of repentance, it produces a damning delusion. Similarly, when the truth of hell fire and judgment is grasped without an accompanying vision of the grace of Calvary, guilt and fear produce alarming destruction in the individual. Jesus came full of both grace and truth—they were balanced in Him.

What Jesus essentially was is what eventually flowed from Him. Dr. Luke records, "All bare him witness, and wondered at the *gracious words* which proceeded out of his mouth..." (Luke 4:22, italics added). Leaving the modifying adjective "gracious," another translation uses the noun form with a modifying prepositional phrase, "the words of grace," to emphasize the fact that the words of Jesus not only imparted information, they imparted grace as well. His person and His words are full of grace. His glory still manifests itself in grace. Many modern Christians have felt His garment of grace brush against them as they have read His gracious words in the sacred script. His grace is tangible; it can be seen and heard, according to John and Paul.

The New Testament writers share an abundance of facts about God's grace, such as:

1) Grace is *receivable:* "By whom we have received grace ..." (Romans 1:5).

2) Grace is the *agent of justification:* "Being justified freely by his grace ..." (Romans 3:24).

3) Grace is the *agent of salvation:* "... (by grace ye are saved)...."

For by grace are ye saved through faith; and that not of yourselves: it is the gift of God: Not of works, lest any man should boast" (Ephesians 2:5, 8, 9).

4) Grace is *accessible:* "By whom also we have access by faith into this grace wherein we stand . . ." (Romans 5:2).

5) Grace *abounds:* ". . . where sin abounded, grace did much more abound" (Romans 5:20).

6) Grace *reigns:* "That as sin hath reigned unto death, even so might grace reign through righteousness unto eternal life by Jesus Christ our Lord" (Romans 5:21).

7) Grace is a *gift:* "I say, through the grace given unto me . . ." (Romans 12:3).

8) Grace is *abundant:* ". . . much more they which receive abundance of grace and of the gift of righteousness shall reign in life by one, Jesus Christ" (Romans 5:17).

9) Grace is *sufficient:* "My grace is sufficient for thee . . ." (2 Corinthians 12:9).

10) Grace is the *channel of God's call:* ". . . that called you into the grace of Christ unto another gospel. . . . God . . . called me by his grace" (Galatians 1:6, 15).

11) Grace is *glorious:* "To the praise of the glory of his grace . . ." (Ephesians 1:6).

12) Grace is *rich:* "In whom we have redemption through his blood, the forgiveness of sins, according to the riches of his grace" (Ephesians 1:7).

13) Grace *can be ministered:* "Let no corrupt communication proceed out of your mouth, but that which is good to the use of edifying, that it may minister grace unto the hearers" (Ephesians 4:29).

14) Grace *accompanies singing:* "Let the word of Christ dwell in you richly in all wisdom; teaching and admonishing one another in psalms and hymns and spiritual songs, singing with grace in your hearts to the Lord" (Colossians 3:16).

15) Grace is *strength:* "Thou therefore, my son, be strong in the grace that is in Christ Jesus" (2 Timothy 2:1).

16) Grace is *God's throne:* "Let us therefore come boldly unto the throne of grace, that we may obtain mercy, and find grace to help in time of need" (Hebrews 4:16).

17) Grace *establishes:* "... For it is a good thing that the heart be established with grace ..." (Hebrews 13:9).

18) Grace is *increasable:* "Grace and peace be multiplied unto you.... But grow in grace ..." (2 Peter 1:2; 3:18).

Surely, then, grace must be much more than "God's love in action" (another popular definition of grace). Grace must be a manifestation of the whole nature of God to man. It is all that God is, made available to affect all that man has become. It is divine resources placed at man's disposal; it is eternal energy flowing into temporal creatures. Grace builds a bridge between time and eternity and narrows the gap between heaven and earth. Grace enables the godless to become Godlike without losing their humanity. Without grace man has no hope of God in this world or in the world to come. Gloriously, "The grace of God ... hath appeared to all men" (Titus 2:11).

How Grace Comes to Man

"Grace be unto you ... from ... Jesus Christ" (Colossians 1:2). The New Testament leaves little doubt about the channel for grace's flow. John agrees with Paul for he wrote, "For the law was given by Moses, but grace and truth came by Jesus Christ" (John 1:17).

Just as law differs from grace, so there is a difference in the manner of imparting each of them. Law came through a man, but grace came through Christ Jesus. We may bring one another under law and regulations, but we cannot impart divine grace to anyone. Christ alone is that channel. Only by relating to Him can we be recipients of His grace.

When God led the children of Israel out of their bondage in the land of Egypt toward the liberty of the Promised Land, He had that nation pause at Mount Sinai while He revealed Himself to them. He offered an intimate relationship to them, but in their fear they expressed a preference for a written code. As professional slaves they were used to obeying orders but were very uncomfortable with warm relationships. So at their request, God gave them law through their human leader, Moses.

Lest we condemn them for choosing the lower when God Himself had offered them the higher, we do well to remember how we, too, are more inclined toward the acceptance of law than we are grace. Most of us have such guilt problems that we are comfortable if law cracks the whip once in a while and if somebody builds a fence around us and says, "You can't do this, you can't do that; you can't go here, and you can't go there." We like to kick our heels, salute, and say, "Yes, sir; yes, sir; I feel much better now that you've told me the boundaries of my limitations."

But God doesn't want to lead His people merely by codes and ethics, by rules and regulations, by limitations, by imposition of a hard and fast law, rule, or command. Instead, God wants to lead His people with His presence, with that soft-spoken inner voice, and He wants a response of faith, not of fear. He wants us to respond to the commander, not to a command. He is interested that we be recipients, not of law, per se, but of grace in the person of the Lord Jesus Christ. From the moment Christ was revealed to men they began to be the recipients of grace in a magnitude unheard of in the Old Testament, for Jesus Christ is God's channel of grace; it flows from Him abundantly. Those who learn how to come into fellowship with Him find themselves in a flow of grace that baffles explanation.

Revelation of Grace

Constantly throughout the history of the Church, Christ has revealed Himself to an individual, or a group of individuals, and this revelation birthed a fresh relationship with the Lord. Out of this vital relationship, almost as a by-product of it, came a fresh flow of grace.

From our position in history, and with our capacity for hindsight, we're tempted to declare that it was at that moment that a new doctrine was introduced to the Church. But it was not a doctrine these individuals came into; it was a flow of the grace of God that transformed their lives, illuminated their spiritual understanding, and gave them fresh impetus to move higher in the things of God. It is usually subsequent generations who make a doctrine out of someone else's experience of grace.

Quite consistently, when a person comes into a vital flow of the grace of God others gravitate to him, desiring to share in the divine life and to learn from the teacher. But try as he will, he cannot pass on the grace he has received. He may communicate principles, concepts, and theology, but he cannot impute the divine grace that has so radically affected his life. His followers will do everything possible to transfer this grace to a second generation. They will reduce his teachings and exhortations to writing, codify his behavior patterns, and reduce his spiritual behavior to rules and regulations. They may even form schools to teach these things to others, who, in turn, enter the ministry to train believers in these principles and sometimes this process escalates into the formation of another Christian denomination. Usually it takes two or three generations to discover that what has been transmitted is another set of laws, not the flow of divine grace.

Needed: A Personal Confrontation With Jesus

We cannot transmit divine life to another. Each succeeding generation needs a new relationship with the Lord Jesus Christ, and each individual in our generation must have a personal encounter with the Lord Jesus if he is to experience the grace of God in his life.

We may buy the tapes of one who flows in God's grace; read his books; attend his conferences; learn to act as he acts. We may memorize his principles and even acquire his vocabulary, but we cannot have what he has unless we, too, go to the Source and drink freely from the fountain of grace. "Grace came by Jesus Christ" (*see* John 1:17).

How careful we should be in dealing with people under conviction of sin. Sometimes when a person with a totally messed-up life responds to an altar call, weeping because of the weight of guilt and unresolved inner conflict, he is met by a personal worker who seeks to determine the nature of the problem. In coming to grips with that problem he sometimes is able to give guidance that resolves it and brings great inner relief to the penitent. Unfortunately, this may eventually damn that individual to an eternal hell because he accepts the solving of his problem as the conversion process and is thereby immunized from any further convicting work of the Spirit. No matter how efficiently we may solve men's problems, whether at an altar of prayer, in a counseling room, or in the legislatures of America, none is converted until he has met Jesus. One alarming situation in America's churches is the high percentage of people who come back again, but have not been born again. We have taught them to conform to our ways, but they have not been transformed by God's Spirit. They get integrated into our programs, but they are never initiated into a relationship with our Founder, the Lord Jesus Christ. They are convinced but not converted.

Religious Law = Spiritual Insecurity

Those who are dependent upon observance of rules and codes for their salvation live in perpetual insecurity, for they have convinced themselves that it is what they do, not what Christ has already done, that secures their eternal destiny. Their awareness of heaven's rewards varies from day to day and from emotional level to emotional level. They are much like the Old Testament saints who had to depend upon animal sacrifices for the expiation of their sins. These sacrifices for sin were offered daily, and yet even the high priest feared to enter into the presence of God on the Day of Atonement.

No matter how faithfully we may observe law, it cannot afford us much security, for at any moment we may break one of the laws and be guilty of them all. That is the height of insecurity!

Christ's Grace = Inner Peace

After His Resurrection, Jesus consistently told His disciples, "Peace be unto you . . ." (John 20:21), and it is still His greeting to those who encounter Him. He has fulfilled the law for us (Matthew 5:17), redeemed us from the curse of the law (Galatians

3:13 and 4:5), and has become the channel through which God's grace is made available to us. Now it is "by grace are ye saved through faith; and that not of yourselves: it is the gift of God" (Ephesians 2:8). God did not choose to manifest grace through the written Word, but through the Living Word.

If grace could come to man through religious organizations, rules, or ritual, it certainly should have been manifested in the days of the tabernacle in the wilderness, but it wasn't. Those were days of divine law. Grace is available only through Jesus Christ, not even through the preaching of Jesus. But if that preaching succeeds in bringing individuals into an intimate relationship with Jesus, they will experience a flow of grace that almost defies adequate description. One may say that grace seems to flow like a river; another may declare that God's grace is the very spiritual atmosphere breathed in heavenly places. Others have declared that grace was like blood coursing through their spiritual being. When we are in the presence of the Lord Jesus Christ everything we see, hear, feel, or sense seems to be permeated with God's grace. We come out of that presence filled with grace, not with guilt. We live in faith, not in fear; we're filled with joy, not judgment, when we have been exposed to God's great grace. No wonder Paul's salutatory prayer couples grace and peace. They are as inseparable as sunlight and warmth, for the second is a result of the first.

3

Jesus, Source of Peace

"Grace be unto you, and peace, from God our Father and the Lord Jesus Christ" (Colossians 1:2).

It has been suggested that Paul's inclusion of "peace" in his salutation was merely a carry-over from his Hebrew heritage where *shalom* (peace) was, and still is, a rather standard greeting among Jews. Nonetheless, since he was writing to Gentiles and was using the Greek language, this is highly improbable. More likely he coupled grace and peace to show that peace is a progressive outgrowth of God's grace. Grace must, of necessity, pave the way for the coming of peace.

Peace: The Outflow of Grace

As Israel quickly learned, the law does not remove wickedness; it merely reveals it. The law says, "Do this and live," and "If you don't do it, divine wrath will come upon you," but it does not energize or enable a person to do or to refrain from doing. In its constant revelation of our wrongs, failings, and inconsistencies, it produces an inner turmoil, frustration, and anger. Well did Isaiah write, "There is no peace, saith my God, to the wicked" (Isaiah 57:21).

This is true whether we are wickedly religious, trying to be sinless through observance of days, codes, and ordinances, or whether we are wickedly irreligious, seeking to escape inner condemnation by ignoring the rules imposed by God. All wickedness disturbs the harmonious relationship between God and man, thereby forfeiting all sense of rest and contentment. Sin always destroys serenity, and perversity prevents peace. That's why peace issues from the Lord Jesus Christ, who was given to men as God's answer to the sin question. His infinite grace channels divine peace into the tumultuous human spirit. As another has said, "Grace is the fountain from which peace flows as a stream" (Isaiah 48:18, Lockyer: *All the Doctrines of the Bible*).

Peace: A Gift of Jesus

It is unlikely that Paul knew much peace until he met Jesus. By his own testimony he was a Judaizer and a zealot, earnestly endeavoring to satisfy an inner craving by his faithful observance of the law. He also invested himself in higher education, graduating from the school of Gamaliel, in his obvious search for contentment. Religiously he was a Pharisee, as was his father before him; politically he seems to have been a member of the Sanhedrin; socially he was either a bachelor (which would have prevented his membership in the Sanhedrin), or his marriage had broken up, but either way he lacked domestic tranquility. He was a seeker, a doer, and a joiner, but there is no evidence of inner peace in his life. Quite the opposite, for his violent activity as a persecutor of the Church reveals a stormy, warlike nature erupting from within this highly educated man. For all of his education, dedication, zeal, and political position, Paul had not tasted inner peace until his conversion on the Damascus road, because, as he writes here, Jesus is our Source of peace, and until He is embraced as the complete fulfillment of the law for our individual lives, there can be no peace.

Peace: Associated With Chastisement

The concept of Jesus' being the Source of peace is not restricted to the New Testament. Isaiah declared, "For unto us a child is born . . . and his name shall be called Wonderful, Counsellor, The mighty God, The everlasting Father, The *Prince* of *Peace*" (Isaiah 9:6, italics added). He is the Prince of Peace; that is His domain; He rules over peace and is in charge of it. That's His title; that's His name; that's His revelation: Peace!

The mature parent in the home is the source of peace for the household. When the children lose their peaceful relationships with one another it often requires the intervention of mother or father to settle the "war" and restore peace. If the discord in the children brings them into a violation of the laws of the home, peace cannot be restored until the rebellion is broken and the guilt for that behavior is remitted. Quite often the child who cannot be talked or bribed back to peace can be chastened into it, for the punishment seems to remit the guilt; he or she has paid the price and the issue is settled.

The fundamental law of life, that guilt must be remitted and settled before peace can return, does not cease when these children mature into parenthood. No matter what our age, our violation must be handled or the guilt will never go away. In the matter of our guilt before God, it is impossible for us to accept the penalty for our actions because, "The wages of sin is death . . ." (Romans 6:23). So God chastened Jesus for us, not as our whipping boy but as "the second man" (1 Corinthians 15:47), whom God accepted as a representative for the whole human race. Isaiah also spoke of this when he wrote, ". . . the chastisement of our peace was upon him . . ." (Isaiah 53:5). Christ was not beaten with the Roman cat-o'-nine-tails thirty-nine times just to make healing available for our bodies; He was chastened so we could be brought back to peace with ourselves, with one another, and with God.

Peace: Aid to Health

However, His stripes purchased healing for the whole man, but God works from within to without: from the spirit to the body. When our spirit/soul comes into peace, our body often comes into health, because one of the major causes of sickness is lack of inner peace.

Some years ago a doctor told me that 90 percent of people's illnesses are from the ears up. He assured me that he didn't mean they were imagined or psychosomatic, but that genuine organic malfunctions were produced as the result of strain, pressure, frustration, and fear. The loss of inner tranquility induced violent physical reactions.

My oldest daughter, Dorothy, is a nurse and for a while worked for a Christian doctor in Phoenix, Arizona. She was extremely pleased with his manner with the patients, his lab work, and his diagnostic skills, but initially she was shocked by the prescriptions he wrote. Repeatedly, he would have her join him in his office with the patient after the diagnosis was completed. Hastily writing on a prescription pad, he would tear the prescription off, hand it to the patient, and say, "This prescription will cure your symptoms. Now I would like to get to the cause of your sickness. Whom do you hate?"

Shocked, the patient quickly denied any such emotion.

"But our tests indicate that you are filled with deep negative emotions," the doctor continued. "Do you resent someone, or feel that you have been used unfairly?"

It usually took some gentle pressure to get the patient to open his emotions to the doctor, but when he did, the good doctor reached for his prescription pad and jotted down several Scripture verses with the instruction that they be read three times daily. Then the doctor asked Dorothy to make a future appointment for the patient to return for another prescription of God's Word.

We hardly need to be told that his rate of cures was amazingly high. He was treating the whole man, fully aware that a wounded spirit or a hate-filled soul pollutes the entire system. "Bring inner peace and produce outer health," seemed to be his philosophy.

Because Christ became our Representative in being chastened for sin we can, by identifying with Him, enter into the peace of God and find wholeness for our entire being.

Peace: More Than the Absence of Oppressive Circumstances

Too often we miss the peace of God because we think peace is the absence of oppressive circumstances. We speak of the waveless sea as peaceful, and view the meandering brook crawling slowly through the meadow as a peaceful scene. This is, of course, descriptive of our inner feelings when peace prevails, but peace is not the absence of action.

During World War II a contest was held for artists throughout America. They were invited to submit one of their paintings that best depicted peace. Sunsets, flowing streams, snowcapped mountains, and pastoral scenes poured in abundantly, but the first prize was awarded to a very different scene. This picture showed a raging storm over a narrow valley. To the left, a waterfall cascaded down a sheer bluff while lightning streaked across the blackened sky. Growing precariously from the sheer face of the cliff was a small scrub tree, its few surviving branches bending yieldingly to the pressure of the wind. Perched on one of these limbs that protruded over the waterfall was a small bird, its head turned upward in defiance of the pounding rain, singing at the top of its voice. In spite of all the turmoil around it, it still had a song and sang it. That's peace! Inward peace defies outward circumstances.

How often in the counseling room do we hear, "I'm unable to cope with my circumstances any longer. My ungodly husband (or wife) makes life so unbearable that I'm about to crack up. I want you to pray that God will deliver me from this marriage."

What they probably are expressing is a death wish, but even if God did slay their impossible mates they wouldn't have peace; they would only have a change of problems. Peace is not determined by another's actions but by our relationship to the Prince of Peace. "Great peace have they which love thy law: and nothing shall offend them" (Psalms 119:165), is the promise of God's Word.

Peace: A Result of Relationship

Since peace is a result of our relationship to Jesus Christ who, the Scripture declares, "is our peace" (Ephesians 2:14), it is neither produced nor reduced by the state of our marriage, our financial situation, or our health. Because it has a divine source, it is not diluted or polluted by human circumstances. It remains constant.

Several years ago, my wife and I had an opportunity to prove this in our personal lives. When I was pastoring in Eugene, Ore-

gon, I was in the midst of conducting a board meeting at the con-
clusion of our Thursday-evening worship service when an insistent
knock on the door interrupted us. One of the board members
opened the door to reveal an ashen-faced member of the congregation who, without any formal greeting, cried, "Come quickly, pastor. There has been a tragic automobile accident involving your
daughter." With that she leaned against the door casing in a
slouch, obviously emotionally distressed at what she had just seen.

I rushed into the church auditorium where my wife was playing
the piano and told her the bad news, and together we went to the
scene of the accident to view the most mangled mess we had ever
seen. Our youngest daughter, while driving her Volkswagen home
from the service with her fiancé as her passenger, had stopped at
an intersection, awaiting an opportunity to make a left turn, when
a drunken driver swerved his jeep at over sixty miles an hour right
into the front of the little "bug," caving it in on the two young
people, mangling and mashing them into bloody pulps.

Eleanor, my wife, and I looked at one another, each awaiting the
collapse of the other, but in the midst of the horror both of us became aware of an inner peace. The Spirit whispered within me,
"Take this like a man; it's not out of control; it's from Me."

Leaning toward my wife, I shared what the Spirit had impressed
upon me. "We'll just have to accept it as from His hand, then," she
said.

We followed the ambulance to the hospital and spent a long
night waiting in the emergency room while the doctors did what
they could to save our daughter's life. Loving members of our congregation poured through the waiting room, offering us comfort
and solace, but we were amazed to find ourselves ministering comfort and assurance to them.

About three in the morning, after the last member of the congregation had left us, my wife asked me, "Honey, would it be
disrespectful if I curled up in this chair and went to sleep? I'm so
tired." And sleep she did. When one of the attending doctors came
out of surgery to report on the condition of our Tina, he called
loudly, "Nurse!"

"What's wrong?" I asked.

"Your wife has collapsed," he replied; "she may have gone into shock."

"Relax," I told him. "She hasn't fainted; she's merely taking a nap."

During the following days, while Tina's life hung in the balance, we were virtually bathed in a peace that was totally disconnected from our circumstances. We refused to let people pour out sympathy upon us, or even get earnestly involved in prayer over us. We didn't take time out from our duties or miss a single preaching session. Hadn't the Lord told us that it was not out of control?

Sometimes it looked as though it were. Two young people requiring such intensive care can run up a hospital bill that is nearly astronomical, and to further challenge me I discovered that the man who had caused all of this suffering did not have a cent of insurance and refused to offer any financial assistance. My only recourse was to sue him for damages, but the Spirit continually impressed upon me, "Don't sue. Your testimony in this town is worth far more than any settlement you might get."

On the surface it seemed that we might lose our daughter, every earthly asset we possessed, and be strapped with medical bills for the rest of our natural lives. Still my heart continued to sing the words of the beautiful Gospel song, "Peace, peace, wonderful peace; coming down from the Father above. . . ."

Mentally, I was grappling with circumstances beyond my control; emotionally I was torn between my desire for my daughter to live and the doctors' opinions that her chances were slim and decreasing daily; physically I was exhausted from the strain; but spiritually I had a peace "which passeth all understanding . . ." (Philippians 4:7).

In the great mercy of God, my daughter miraculously recovered and returned to work at the hospital; the young man healed completely; all bills were paid in full; this young couple married and now reside in Argentina. But the first miracle in this series of miracles was the deep, abiding, prevailing peace that God gave to my wife and me.

Perhaps too much Christian energy is expended praying for situations and circumstances to change. Probably we should stop try-

ing to twist God's arm with our desperate pleas and invest our time
and energy to develop a relationship with Jesus so, like the disciples, we can receive peace in the midst of the storm. When He is
ready to stop the storm He will. If we will honestly examine our
past walk with God, we'll have to admit that it has always required
pressure to move us from one level of relationship to another. The
higher we rise, the more pressure it takes. We need trials, storms,
and troubles to squeeze us out of the lower into the higher, for
pain, pressure, and problems are part of the process God uses to
produce a more intimate walk with God. But while all this is in
progress, we need not lose our peace. Peace flourishes in the midst
of those circumstances, for they are but tools of God to bring us
unto Himself, from whom peace flows.

Peace: A Universal Provision

That peace is an integral part of the message of the Scriptures is
evidenced by the appearance of the word *peace* more than 425
times in the King James Version of the Bible. Thirty-three Old
Testament books, and every book in the New Testament, except
John's First Epistle, speak of peace. This encompasses a rather
wide range of meaning, since both the Hebrew word *shalom* and the
Greek word *eirēnē* refer variously to concordant relationships between men, between nations, and in the churches. Sometimes these
original words are translated "friendliness," "rest," or "quietness,"
but the most important meaning of *peace* is the harmonized relationships between God and man which have been made available
through the cross of Jesus Christ, and the sense of rest and contentment that results from such reconciled relationships. The Old
Testament pattern of worship even provided for peace offerings,
looking forward to the coming of Jesus, from whom positive relationships with God would be made available, while the New Testament affirms, "And, having made peace through the blood of his
cross . . ." (Colossians 1:20), and, "But now in Christ Jesus ye who
sometimes were far off are made nigh by the blood of Christ. For
he is our peace, who hath made both one, and hath broken down
the middle wall of partition between us; Having abolished in his

flesh the enmity . . . so making peace" (Ephesians 2:13–15).

So universal and all-embracing is the scriptural offering of peace that God is called "the God of peace" (Romans 15:33; 16:20). It is more than a gift or provision He has made; peace is inseparably connected with the person of God. He purchased our peace. He parades, proclaims, and perpetuates that peace. He does not instruct us about peace; He infuses us with peace. He is the Producer; we are the partakers. He is its beginning; we are its beneficiaries. Peace is inherent in God's nature, and is inherited by us when we become obedient sons of God.

Furthermore, the Scriptures connect three distinct prepositions with the word *peace*. We read about peace *with* God (Romans 5:1); the peace *of* God (Colossians 3:15); and peace *from* God (Colossians 1:2). So we have peace above us, peace within us, and peace around us. We have peace in the heavens, peace in the heart, and peace in the home. Our relationships are harmonious in the spirit world, the human world, and the natural world. Peace is profound, yet practical. Peace is positive and propitious, but above all peace is prodigious; it is so immense as to affect the totality of human experience both in time and eternity. Such is the peace that God gives to His saints.

Peace: A Guide and Garrison

In speaking of the practicality of peace, Paul told the saints in Colossae, "Let the peace of God rule in your hearts . . ." (Colossians 3:15). We are not to be ruled by turmoil and confusion, but by peace. "God is not the author of confusion, but of peace . . ." Paul wrote (1 Corinthians 14:33). Some of us have learned to shun anything that disturbs our peace; it becomes a safety check within the believer. If it is of God there should be an inner peace, no matter what the outer circumstances, but if it is not of God, or is contrary to the will of God, there should be a disturbance of our inner tranquility. When that happens it is wise to back up until the peace is restored and try another direction of action. God's peace is present to rule our hearts, to help govern our actions, to act as a Geiger counter in our inner soul and spirit. No action or attitude is worth sacrificing God's deposit of peace. *"Let* the peace of God rule in your hearts." It will not dominate or force itself as the guiding force in our lives; it is more like a whisper or a gentle nudge. We must develop a sensitivity to it and give it a place of guidance in our lives or its value will be lost.

Similarly, Paul speaks of this peace as being the protection of our minds. He wrote, "And the peace of God, which passeth all understanding, shall keep your hearts and minds through Christ Jesus" (Philippians 4:7). The Greek word here translated as "keep" is *phroureō,* which literally means to mount guard as a sentinel, or refers to the station where these soldiers were kept. By implication it means "to hem in; to protect." Accordingly, both the Weymouth and Amplified translations of the New Testament use the word *garrison.* "The peace of God . . . shall *garrison* your hearts and minds. . . ."

What a comfort! In this day when our minds and emotions are attacked hourly by radio, television, the newspapers, and the pressures of everyday living, it is reassuring to know that God has already provided a divine defense for us. God purposed that His peace should garrison itself, make its own home, in our hearts and minds. Before they can be overthrown that peace must be destroyed, for we have been hemmed in and protected by God's peace. Our sanity is never at stake when God's peace is in residence within us. To the Church in Corinth Paul wrote, "We are troubled on every side, yet not distressed; we are perplexed, but not in despair; Persecuted, but not forsaken; cast down, but not destroyed . . ." (2 Corinthians 4:8,9), so great is the protective power of God's peace.

Peace and Prayer

Although peace is a promised gift of God it, like all of God's gifts, must be appropriated and applied to our lives to be effectual. It is not an automatic function, any more than having a house wired for electricity automatically illuminates it. Switches must be turned on. In the matter of receiving divine peace, prayer becomes the switch that allows peace to flow from God to man. Isaiah seemed to realize this for he wrote, "Thou wilt keep him in perfect peace, whose mind is stayed on thee: because he trusteth in thee" (Isaiah 26:3). The praying person chooses to focus his attention on God rather than on himself or his problems and, therefore, enjoys peace when others experience anxiety. Times of private communion with God enable God to share Himself with the worshiper, and He is "the God of peace" (Philippians 4:9).

Throughout the pages of church history men and women who have evidenced outstanding measures of divine peace in their lives have all been persons of much prayer. They learned not only to have a specific prayer time and place but also to communicate with God throughout the rest of the day. Like Jesus they could say, "Father, I thank thee that thou hast heard me. And I knew that thou hearest me always . . ." (John 11:41, 42), so intimate had their relationship become with the Father. In such a posture what could threaten their peace?

When we feel our peace being disturbed, it is time to go to prayer. If we have allowed circumstances to destroy our peace we need to make an altar of prayer until God's peace is reborn in our spirit. The initiative of prayer is ours; and to that extent the option for peace rests with us. Prayer brings peace while prayerlessness often short-circuits the flow of peace from God to man.

Peace: A Person

Prayer brings peace, not because it is a quiet time where tranquility can develop, but because prayer is contact with the Person we call Jesus, and the Scriptures declare that He is the "Prince of Peace" (Isaiah 9:6). True peace is integrally wrapped up in this Person. Jesus is not only the Prince of Peace but He is also the Author of that peace, and He has given that peace to men. "He is our peace" (Ephesians 2:14), is the simple explanation of the Word of God, and nothing can improve on it. Without Him there can be no peace, so the measure of peace in our lives will be in direct proportion to the measure of the life of Jesus that dwells within us. It may take a work of faith to appropriate this successfully, but fortunately Jesus, the Source of our peace, is also the Object of our faith.

4

Jesus, Object of Our Faith

"We give thanks to God and the Father of our Lord Jesus Christ. . . . Since we heard of your faith in Christ Jesus . . ." (Colossians 1:3,4).

Christ Jesus does not impart His peace to make us passive in life; He calms our inner tempests and conquers our terror of God to enable us to become active in the affairs of God's Kingdom. He changes our fear to faith, without which it is impossible to please Him (Hebrews 11:6).

Faith is as divine as God Himself, but it is not God; it is a product of God—just as the shimmering beam of light is a product of the sun. Faith is a divine energy—as real to the spirit world as electricity is to the natural world. Faith is a power, a producing force. It is literal. It is not an attitude, a concept, or merely a doctrine; it is a force. When it is functioning, things happen, but when it is absent we are powerless even to continue what God began, as Peter learned in his attempt to walk on the water (Matthew 14:31).

Faith's Source

Jesus told His disciples, "Have faith in God" (Mark 11:22 RSV). Faith is produced by God, not by man. Faith is a divine energy, not a religious one. It has its origin in the Godhead, not in the Body of Christ. We're not capable of producing this dynamic of faith, only of receiving it. In the same manner that home owners don't produce electricity, but only consume it, we do not produce faith; we only utilize it. Furthermore, the generator that produces electricity does not consume it; it transmits it. Similarly, God does not produce faith to consume it, but to transmit it. We receive faith not to learn how to produce it, but to learn how to release it.

Faith's source is in God the Father, God the Son, and God the Holy Spirit, not in the Bible, not in theology, not in doctrine, although sometimes doctrine is called "the faith." The Bible, theology, and doctrine will direct faith, but will not produce it.

Faith is not even produced by prayer, fasting, or works, though these might release faith. Fasting for faith might produce a weight loss, and working for faith may bring about exhaustion, but faith is not produced by man's efforts; its source is totally in God. "God hath dealt to every man the measure of faith" (Romans 12:3).

Faith is not found in the giving of testimonies, the telling of stories, or the viewing of miracles. We consistently send individuals with outstanding testimonies on the banquet circuit because we want to produce faith. They may inspire existing faith, but testimonies can't produce faith. We look to miracles to produce faith, but miracles are the product, not the producer of faith. In Jesus' day, He demonstrated miracle after miracle, yet these did not produce faith, for Jesus was crucified as a rabble-rousing pretender. All forsook Him, even the recipients of the miracles.

After we receive faith from God, we may indeed go to the Bible, doctrine, or theology for some direction of that faith, or we may find ourselves in prayer, fasting, or works to release that faith. We may even find ourselves involved in testimonies, stories, or miracles that continue to inspire that faith, but we cannot produce it, for its source is in God; it's His faith.

In my book *Let Us Abide* I wrote, "The life of faith is not optional; it is obligatory. It was never offered as an elective for the supersaints. It is not a matter of preference; it is a prerequisite to divine life." Accordingly, few themes in Scripture are more fully developed, for faith is mentioned over three hundred times in the New Testament, and great portions of the Old Testament are devoted to recording the steps God used to impart faith to men of His choosing. Faith, unquestionably, is a most essential impartation from God to man for, as I point out in my book on abiding, "Faith is . . . the source of, or channel for our access to grace, healing, indwelling of Christ, justification, life, promise of the Spirit, propitiation, protection (shield and breastplate), righteousness, salvation, sanctification, standing, strength, steadfastness, understanding, and walk."

But for all of faith's prominence in sacred literature, the Bible does not seek so much to define faith as to channel and direct it.

Faith's Channel

This divine energy called faith which is produced by God must have a channel to bring it from God to man. Paul declares, "So then faith cometh by hearing, and hearing by the word of God" (Romans 10:17). There are two Greek words used frequently in the New Testament for "the Word of God": *Rhema* and *Logos*. *Rhema* fundamentally means "a living word spoken or a word being spoken by a living God." It is the Greek word used for "the Word of God" here in Romans 10:17.

So then, faith cometh by hearing, and hearing by a *Rhema*, a word being spoken by a living God.

The other Greek word used for "the Word of God," *Logos*, basically means "the thing that is being spoken or the thing that is being spoken about." In other words, what God says is a *Logos*, but while God is saying it, it is a *Rhema*. Faith does not come in a *Logos*, but in a *Rhema* while God is talking, while the speaking is going on. That is when faith is being transmitted, for it is coming to us on the voice channel of God. Divine energy accompanies God's voice, and the Bible calls that energy "faith."

Too often we substitute what I call "paper faith" for God's faith. We search out several Bible promises on a common theme, memorize and quote them until we can give mental assent to their validity. Calling this mental exercise "faith" we step out to "claim the promises," only to fail miserably. It is not our speaking the passages of the Bible but the Spirit's speaking it that channels faith. We need a *Rhema*, not merely a *Logos*.

A few years ago, God, through prophecy, told the congregation I was pastoring that the building program we were launching into was not ours, but His, and if we would supply the labor, He would supply the material. For me this was a time of learning to know the voice of God, for He talked to me about board feet, cubic yards of concrete, how many nails to purchase, and also about design. We didn't have a builder and we didn't know how to build, so we had to ask the Lord how, and He told us. That was His teaching process with me.

God more than kept His word to us, for we completed that building, then two additions to it, and finally another building as large as the original one.

In the early stages of our building program, I was guest speaker in a denominational church in Spokane, Washington, where I shared a bit of what God was doing. Subsequently, the pastor asked to be put on our church mailing list to receive our bulletin so he could keep up with our project.

Later, at a camp meeting, I met this pastor outside the auditorium. As I greeted him, he recoiled, upbraided me, and accused me of causing his ruin. Since six years had elapsed, and I had had no further contact with him, I asked him for an explanation, whereupon he said I had bankrupted him. Then he told me his story. "You remember those bulletins you sent? I followed what you were doing step by step. I said, 'If God will do it for Judson Cornwall, He will do it for me.' So we did everything you did. Just before this camp meeting the sheriff repossessed our property; I've lost everything and it is all your fault."

I stepped up to him, hugged him, and said, "My brother, if I had known you were copying me, I'd have flown to your side immediately and said, 'Oh, no; get your own word from God; you can't have my faith.'"

You see, my own blood brother had been in a building program just 120 miles from me, and God's method for him was borrowing money and turning the project over to a builder. While I worked with my knuckles and sweat, putting in long hours, he played golf, but that was God's plan for him, and what I went through was God's plan for me.

We don't dare take another man's word from the Lord as our direction, for God speaks to individuals, and He wants to speak to each of us, for when He speaks faith comes to us. It is hard not to believe God when He's talking, because He totally believes in what He is saying. He's convincing! He's the Supersalesman! When you merely see it in a letter, translated by someone who received it, it's not as easy to have faith in it; for the faith comes not by the translation, but by the speaking.

Some feel that God doesn't speak anymore; they say, "Stop telling people you hear from the Lord; say you have a sense, a feeling, or perhaps are receiving a direction." But over a thousand times in the Bible it says God spoke to man. I don't know of a generation that needs to hear Him more than this generation. God is still speaking; we are just not listening. But if we tuned from Channel Flesh to Channel Spirit, we'd begin to hear again; and when we hear, faith will come to us.

As a certain brother was preaching, the Spirit of the Lord said, "Sit up, Cornwall, and listen; I'm saying something to you." Suddenly, beyond the beautiful and scholarly presentation of the speaker, I could hear the voice of the Holy Spirit and with that hearing came a forceful flow of faith. God wants us to return to hearing His voice, not just the voice of the messenger.

Following a morning service where I had ministered, the people didn't want to leave the auditorium. Finally, because I had an urgent appointment, my driver and I slipped out. Later the pastor reported to us that the people had testified they had become "drunk" on the Word of God, for as the Word came by the Spirit, faith was produced. Faith is intoxicating, exhilarating, and exciting. When it comes we believe unbelievable things, declare things that aren't as though they were, and find ourselves standing alongside those heroes of Hebrews 11 who by faith did what couldn't humanly be done because faith doesn't know it can't be done. This is the faith that comes by hearing the *Rhema* Word of God (Romans 10:17).

The Spirit (which produces the *Rhema*) and the written Word (the *Logos*) always agree. God's original order of creation seems to be His present order of re-creation. We read in Genesis 1:2, ". . . the Spirit of God moved upon the face of the waters," and then in verse 3, "And God said. . . ." The Spirit prepares, then the Word proclaims. God combines the flow of His Spirit with His Word; as He by the Spirit quickens the Word, it is God speaking, and this is the channel of faith.

Many of the errors, failures, and disappointments in faith have been errors of concept. We've said, "If we can believe it we can have it"; "name it, claim it." Not so, for we can have only what the Spirit speaks.

A businessman who claimed he had stepped out on faith by going into business came to me for help because everything seemed to have gone wrong. When I asked if he had received a word from God to go into business, he said no, but that he was just trusting and believing the Lord. He said he felt he could do things without hearing from God. I explained that he could but that he couldn't do them in divine faith.

It's not faith until God says to do it. We can step out into business anytime we want to, but we should declare honestly that we are going to take a chance, for business has an element of gamble in it. Some will never be happy working for others until they find out if they have the capacity to work for themselves. Take the gamble, if you will, but don't blame God if you fail.

But if God says, *Go into business,* you won't fail!

I've seen churches built by "faith" that totally failed because they were built by presumption. But when we move according to God's Word, there is total success, sometimes not as man counts success, but as God declares success.

Until the pages of God's Word speak, they cannot channel faith to us. Faith is not reaching for our desires; it is responding to His speaking. When God speaks, we appropriate the promise, become a participant in the pursuit, and something is performed.

Faith's Object

Furthermore, faith is more than positive emotions or the by-product of religious activity. Often when I am at my lowest ebb, I haven't seen a miracle lately, my current testimony isn't worth telling, I haven't taken time to pray, I haven't fasted, and there have been no recent good works to speak of; when the Word hasn't been doing anything outstanding within me, my theology and doctrine are wavering a bit, and I have no basis for expecting faith, God mercifully opens His Word to me, imparting a believing faith that produces spiritual and natural results. I did not and could not produce it; it was totally the work and gift of God. Therefore I could never become the object of my faith, for during periods when I believe in myself the least God often flows the greatest measure of faith.

Here in Colossians Paul and Timothy speak of rejoicing, "Since we heard of your faith in Christ Jesus . . ." (Colossians 1:4). They were not exuberant because the Colossians had developed positive thinking or "saving faith," but "faith in Christ Jesus." Jesus is not only the Source of our faith but is the Object of that faith. It originates in Him and must return to Him. "Jesus is the author and finisher of our faith," Paul says (*see* Hebrews 12:2).

During our Christian walk in this life, we very often do not have faith for the solving of specific problems, but we can have faith in Jesus. Because we have received the faith of God, we can "believe that God is, and that He is the rewarder of them that diligently seek Him" (*see* Hebrews 11:6). We may be as impotent as the disciples in calming storms, but we need not join them in their anxious fears, for Christ is in the boat with us, and we trust Him to do what is right. He can either calm the storm, make the boat unsinkable, or give us great swimming ability, but any way He chooses to handle the emergency will be good, for God is a good God, and everything He does is inherently good.

We may not have faith for the salvation of a loved one, but we can have faith in Jesus the Saviour. We can be weak in faith for the healing of sick bodies but strong in our faith in Jesus the healer. The need is not the object of our faith; Jesus is. The faith we have received from God has to go beyond what needs to be produced to the Producer Himself, for He is the Source of our supply, not our attitude, concept, or religious exercise. Our faith is in a Person, not a problem. Our confidence is in Christ, not a crisis. We do not look to natural resources, spiritual energies, human ingenuity, or personal power for the answer to our pressing, perplexing problems.

We look to Jesus. It is He who has promised, "But seek ye first the kingdom of God, and his righteousness; and all these things shall be added unto you" (Matthew 6:33). We are not told to ignore the need but to turn to the Source of supply. "My God shall supply all your need according to his riches in glory *by Christ Jesus*" (Philippians 4:19, italics added).

When people declare that they have no faith while God's Word declares, ". . . God hath dealt to every man the measure of faith" (Romans 12:3), it usually evidences that they have a wrong concept of faith's object. They are trying to have faith in circumstances in life, usually to change them, when they should have faith in a loving, gracious God who controls the lives of His children. Faith in God should be as natural to a true believer as faith in a father is natural to a son. Unless the father consistently violates his word, this childish faith will mature and strengthen as the son matures. The more the father is found to be trustworthy, the greater will be the level of the son's faith in him.

The Bible is liberally sprinkled with the testimonies of men and women who proved the faithfulness of God. The entire eleventh chapter of Hebrews is dedicated to such affirmations. God never fails His people. God's promises are always fulfilled (although not always on our time schedule). God's Word is inviolate and cannot lie; neither can God's divine nature enter into deceit. God does not tease or tantalize us. If He says it, He will do it. He redeems His pledges, performs His promises, and projects His unchangeable nature to us. That is why we can trust Him totally, have complete confidence in Him, and fearlessly flow our faith to Him. He is an unfailing Object of our faith. Men will fail us, doctrines may deceive us, and religion often disappoints us, but God never fails.

In the midst of the depression, in the days of my youth, my father's congregation loved to sing the gospel song *God Is Still on the Throne*. Its chorus went:

God is still on the throne, and He will remember His own;
Though trials may press us and burdens distress us, He never
   will leave us alone;

God is still on the throne, and He never forsaketh His own;
His promise is true, He will not forget you, God is still on the
throne.

Each of us must daily reckon with the contrast between our natural life and our spiritual life; between the world's philosophy and
the Bible's philosophy. Unless we are diligently watchful, worldly
standards become Christian standards just by the sheer weight of
their appearance in our lives. This interchange is especially dam-
aging in the realm of our faith. America's standard of measure-
ment for success is things. We seem to have a passion for possessions. The acquiring of money, merchandise, or property seems to
be the motivation for most of our lives. Unfortunately, this philosophy is frequently transferred to our application of God's faith. We
hear a great deal about "having faith for . . .," and the bottom line
is "things." Some even go so far as to categorize their faith, declaring that they have "healing faith," "saving faith," "faith for finances," "faith for business dealings," and so on, which makes
about as much sense as saying we have "refrigerating electricity"
or "vacuuming electricity." In their very definitions they have declared that things are the object of their faith, but the Bible calls
for Jesus to be the Object of that faith. One faith—the faith of
God—is sufficient to meet all of our needs if we keep Jesus as the
Object of that faith.

One of the oft-requested congregational songs during my years
of pastoring was *Living by Faith.* The chorus went:

> Living by faith in Jesus above,
> Trusting, confiding in His great love;
> From all harm safe in His sheltering arm,
> I'm living by faith and feel no alarm.

Isn't this basically what Peter was saying when he wrote concerning Jesus, "Who by him do believe in God, that raised him up
from the dead, and gave him glory; *that your faith and hope might be in
God*" (1 Peter 1:21, italics added)?

That person who has learned to make Christ Jesus the Object of his faith will never be faithless or hopeless. Neither will he live a loveless existence, since faith and love are inseparable: ". . . faith which worketh by love" (Galatians 5:6).

5

Jesus, Source of Love

"We give thanks to God. . . . Since we heard of your . . . love which ye have to all the saints" (Colossians 1:3,4).

"Since we heard of your faith in Christ Jesus, and of the love which ye have to all the saints" (Colossians 1:4), pinpoints two elements which, if seen in the believer, can do much for the Kingdom of God, since faith is being released back to Christ and love is being released to the saints, and to a needy world.

Faith and Love Are Inseparable

Many times we tend to separate what God has united; while the Kingdom of God is called to unify, we are forever insisting on diversifying it. One way we do this is by taking doctrinal truths and separating them because we think this makes them easier to be understood. To separate for the sake of study is one thing but to separate for the sake of application is another. Because the Scriptures link faith and love so often, we should not separate them, but consider the power they have when used correctly together. Over a dozen times in the New Testament these two words, *faith* and *love,* appear in the same verse.

In 1 Thessalonians 5:8 the admonition is to "put on the breastplate of faith and love," and in Ephesians 6:14 we are bidden to "Stand . . . having on the breastplate of righteousness." Therefore, we must note that the righteousness called for here is defined as faith and love. Since the breastplate is a vital defense for the vulnerable area of our body, we conclude it is very important that we be righteous, and righteousness is a right relationship first with God, second with myself, and third, with others in the body of Christ; thereby we are equipped to withstand in the evil day (Ephesians 6:13).

Several times in the Song of Solomon, which is a prophetic poem on the love relationship between Christ and His bride, there is mention made of the beauty of the bride's breasts. For purposes of provision, nourishment, comfort, and strength, the bride of Christ is to be well developed in the bosom area, i.e., her faith and love should be fully developed, just as that of a mature woman in the natural.

Some churches are very strong on faith but they don't have much love; others have a great deal of love, but they don't have enough faith to handle the church budget. Both extremes are badly out of balance; neither has the perfect symmetry of a beautiful, fully developed woman. God wants His Church to have equal development in the areas of faith and love.

When it is noted that God is developing faith or love in His Church, some say, "Isn't it wonderful that God is finally calling out His Church?" No; He's had His Church all along, but now He's emphasizing the need of full development in these areas. God allows a group to go just so far in the faith realm; then He does not allow further development until His dealings begin to produce a flow of love. Or conversely, in the people who flow so well in love—but not so much in faith—He cuts off the love and deals in the development of faith, so there will not be a lopsided presentation of His Kingdom; for God is a God of balance.

Galatians 5:6 gives me a clue why it is necessary to have faith and love in balance, for ". . . faith . . . worketh by love." If our faith is to produce results, it must be done through the ministration of love.

When we are strong in faith and weak in love, faith does not have a proper channel to work through. This is probably why we see some very awkward things produced by men of faith who have not love. Some are always calling for "equal time" to preach their ideas, but God is calling for "equal development" for adequate presentation of His Gospel.

The Source of Love

Faith and love have a common source in Jesus. We can receive faith and we can also receive love, both from Jesus; however, we cannot produce them from self-effort.

Jesus came from the Father and we know the attributes of the Godhead were expressed in Jesus during His earthly walk. Scores of verses telling of the love of God can easily be located with the help of a concordance. In 1 John 4:16 we note that "God is love. . . ." Further, 2 Corinthians 13:11 calls Him "the God of love." Romans 5:8 explains that "God commendeth his love toward us, in that, while we were yet sinners, Christ died for us." So love was a gift the Father gave to us when He gave us Jesus.

According to Galatians 5:22, the first fruit of the Holy Spirit produced within us is love. How wonderful it is to see it blossom. Some people get so excited at the blossoming that they call it their salvation experience. (So few of us really understand our salvation experience because so many things happen simultaneously—it's hard to sort them out theologically.) But the fact remains—when we meet Jesus, the fruit of love begins to grow, flow, and show. A change takes place in the life. Paul told how it happened to him— the things he once hated he now loved; whereas he had once hated God, he now loved Him. Faith in Christ Jesus had produced love.

So Jesus was a manifestation of God's love. "In this was manifested the love of God toward us, because that God sent his only begotten Son into the world, that we might live through him" (1 John 4:9). "God so loved the world, that he gave his only begotten Son . . ." (John 3:16).

God didn't choose to give us worldly possessions to show His love to mankind, but He chose to give us Jesus, who is the total embodiment of all that God is.

The Nature of Love

The majority of mankind can't yet accept the manifestation of God's love. Instead they call kindness, physical attraction, or lust "love" and thereby leave themselves bereft of the love of God which redeems and satisfies.

We Anglo-Saxons call many things "love" but New Testament Greek specifies degrees of love such as divine love, brotherly kindness, or erotic love; much of the world understands only the latter two degrees of love.

We Christians many times fall short in our understanding of *agape* love, God's divine love as revealed in Jesus.

A few years ago as I knelt to pray, I voiced these words to the Lord: "O Lord, I love You; I love You more than anything in life," and the Lord asked, *What do you mean "love"? This morning your little dog came in to help wake you up and you scratched his head and said, "O Belshazer, I love you." Do you love Me like you love your dog? You told your wife you loved her coffee; do you love Me like coffee? Remember how you hugged your wife after breakfast and said, "Honey, I love you"; do you love Me as you love Eleanor? Or, do you love Me as you love your car, which you patted tenderly as you backed it out the driveway? When you arrived at church, you stood in the parking lot and said, "I just love this building!" Do you love Me the way you love a church building? What do you mean, son?*

I confessed to the Lord that I didn't know what I meant.

Then the Holy Spirit began to pray through me, audibly and inaudibly, for about an hour. Even when I didn't know what He was saying I sensed everything He was trying to express, because there was a breaking up of the fountains of the deep, and love was flowing. I recognized that it had a source from without me; it was healing, strengthening, and then lifting and exciting. When the Holy Spirit had finished praying through me, God said, *Now that is what I call "love."*

The youth of our nation have generated a cry for love; their slogan has been "love"; yet in practice they have given themselves to lust, thus destroying themselves and almost disqualifying themselves from ever knowing what love is. Putting the word *love* on physical attraction and lustful actions that are void of depth or meaning has created human wreckage.

We must meet the Source of love before we can ever know real love. Marriages attempt to function without love, so there is only emptiness. Even Christian marriages are in trouble because an earthly level of sensual attraction is no basis for a flow of God's love from partner to partner.

. The "more excellent way" of 1 Corinthians 12:31, the way of God's love as described in the thirteenth chapter, is the answer to the love problem.

The nine ingredients of divine love are:

1. *Patience:* "Love suffereth long" (*see* 1 Corinthians 13:4). Love is not in a hurry; it bears and hopes and knows things will come out all right; it loves in the midst of negative reaction.

2. *Kindness:* "Love . . . is kind" (*see* 1 Corinthians 13:4). This is love in action, but it never acts rashly or harshly, and is not inconsistent with itself. All things are done in kindness when divine love is flowing as can be seen from the earthly life of Jesus, whose love was active and kind in every instance.

3. *Generosity:* "Love envieth not" (*see* 1 Corinthians 13:4). This is love in competition. We live in a world of competition, but when real love comes up against competition, it is neither jealous nor does it strive to show its superiority.

4. *Humility:* "Love vaunteth not itself, is not puffed up" (*see* 1 Corinthians 13:4). This is love in hiding. Divine love has no parade, no airs; it doesn't do anything that causes it to get the limelight. It works, then retires.

5. *Courtesy:* "Love doth not behave itself unseemly" (*see* 1 Corinthians 13:5). This is love in society; it is always polite and is at home with all classes of people. It is never rude or snobbish.

6. *Unselfishness:* "Love seeketh not her own" (*see* 1 Corinthians 13:5). This is love in essence. It is never selfish or sour; is never bitter. It speaks only the good of others, doesn't retaliate, nor does it seek revenge.

7. *Good Temper:* "Love is not easily provoked" (*see* 1 Corinthians 13:5). This is love in the disposition. It is never irritated or resentful. It is able to handle the person who is out of sorts without becoming out of sorts. It finds it unnecessary to react to actions, for love is good-tempered.

8. *Righteousness:* "Love rejoiceth not in iniquity, but rejoiceth in the truth" (*see* 1 Corinthians 13:6). This is love in its conduct. It is never glad when others go wrong and is always gladdened by goodness in others and to others. It is slow to expose and eager to believe the best.

9. *Sincerity:* "Love beareth all things, believeth all things, hopeth all things, endureth all things" (*see* 1 Corinthians 13:7). Here is love in profession. It is not a hypocrite; it leaves no impression but what is strictly true; is just and joyful; knows how to be silent; and is full of trust.

These ingredients of divine love make life livable between husbands and wives, between parents and children, and between employers and employees.

The Channel of Love

This love of God is to be shown to one another. Jesus said, "A new commandment I give unto you, That ye love one another; as I have loved you, that ye also love one another. By this shall all men know that ye are my disciples, if ye have love one to another" (John 13:34,35).

Love is not always the trademark of a Christian, but it is always the hallmark of a disciple. A flow of love of magnitude great enough to stir the world can only come through those who have heard Jesus' voice and have been willing to leave their "nets" and follow Him in discipleship to be molded or shaped into His divine plan and program. The world watches love flowing from disciple to disciple and knows who is for real, while they just as easily discern shallow Christians.

A disciple doesn't keep love on deposit to collect interest, but releases it to those who need it. He washes feet; he gives of himself in love to other disciples as the need may arise. In being disciples of our Lord Jesus Christ, we can do no less than He did, and that includes loving a lost world with Calvary love.

If He can't love through us, He has no channel to love through; if we will not allow ourselves to be channels of love to our unsaved family members and friends, there is no possible way for God to get love to them.

The Objects of Love

We can learn precious lessons of love in the First Epistle of John. First John 4:7 states, "Beloved, let us love one another: for love is of

God. . . ." But there is further admonition on loving in 1 John 5:1-3: "Whosoever believeth that Jesus is the Christ is born of God: and every one that loveth him that begat loveth him also that is begotten of him. By this we know that we love the children of God, when we love God, and keep his commandments. For this is the love of God, that we keep his commandments: and his commandments are not grievous."

As disciples, our love should flow in three directions: to the Godhead, to the children of God, and to the commandments of God.

In recent years, the Church has been afflicted with self-love and program love but it is time we started loving the Godhead once again. According to this passage, if we love the Father who begat, and the only begotten Son, we will also love His children. First John 4:11 states, "Beloved, if God so loved us, we ought also to love one another [God's kids]." For it is doubtful that we can love God, whom we have not seen, if we can't love our brothers and sisters in Christ. But if we will love one another, we will see the Father and the Son in the faces of other disciples, and we will thereby learn to love God.

Sometimes we build up false images of what a person must look like, then when we meet him, we are disillusioned. When we pray, perhaps we visualize what Jesus looks like. But the Father wants us to love our fellow disciples, and thereby we will see the face of God as we look on their faces.

If we are to know divine love, we must not only love the Godhead, for 1 John 4:20 states: "If a man say, I love God, and hateth his brother, he is a liar: for he that loveth not his brother whom he hath seen, how can he love God whom he hath not seen?"

And we are going to love the commandments of God by keeping them. They are not grievous but are uplifting, strengthening, and edifying. Jesus said as recorded in John 14:15, "If you love me, keep my commandments."

Some of the practical commandments of the Word of God include, "Husbands, love your wives . . ." (Ephesians 5:25); "Fathers, provoke not your children to wrath . . ." (Ephesians 6:4); and "Children, obey your parents in the Lord . . ." (Ephesians 6:1).

A big problem even in Christian homes is a sense of competition in relationships instead of completion. Husbands and wives compete with each other for the affection of the children, for the dollar, for the car, for abilities, for spiritual realms. Jesus did not plan this when He made woman from man; He made her to complete man. In a Latin translation of Genesis, Adam's "help meet" is translated "alter ego"—the other self—the mirror image—that which completes. When God's goal that woman complete man is reached in the love relationship, He is glorified and God's love is shown to the children and the neighbors and friends.

The day a husband discovers that his wife has a deposit of Christ in her is the day he can begin to flow love to her. Likewise parents can detect a deposit of Christ in their children and can love them deeply and completely in the Lord.

As disciples, even in the family unit in the home, love one another, great things will be accomplished for God's Kingdom.

We can love the unlovely as the love of Christ flows through us to them. If we work on the human level we choose the objects of our love carefully; but if we operate on the divine level, we will have enough love to let it flow anywhere there is a recognized deposit of Christ in the heart. His love can flow through us without limit or measure and with no form of penalty.

Perhaps our love will be rejected; but it's His love that is being rejected, if we are allowing it to flow through us. I am not vulnerable when I am loving with His love; He's vulnerable. What more can they do to Him? They pulled the hair off His chin, put a crown of thorns on His head, striped His back with the cat-o'-nine-tails, punctured His hands and His feet, spat upon Him, cursed, mocked, and scoffed Him, ran a spear into His side; and yet He loves, for He is the Source of love. We have received His great love and must pass it on to others.

If we have seen Jesus, we can do this.

6

Jesus, Our Hope

"For the hope which is laid up for you in heaven, whereof ye heard before in the word of the truth of the gospel" (Colossians 1:5).

During the nearly forty years of our marriage, my wife frequently has interchanged the word *hope* for *wish*. If I make a positive statement of fact, her response is often, "Well, I hope so," but her tone is unbelieving. She doesn't "hope" in the Bible sense of the word; she wishes, for she doesn't believe what has been said, nor does she expect it to happen, although she wishes I were right, for the results would be better.

She is not a cynic, nor is she lacking in an understanding of the English language. She merely used the word the way it is used so widely in America. We have watered down the word until, at best, it is anemic, and at worst, it is totally dead, but in the New Testament *hope* is a powerful, living word.

When Paul wrote, "For the hope which is laid up for you in heaven ..." (Colossians 1:5), he used the Greek word *elpis* for "hope." Consistently in the New Testament this word is used in the sense of favorable and confident anticipation of good, and it denotes a contented and joyful expectation of the future and the unseen (Romans 8:24, 25). This is a far cry from "I wish it were so," or "I'll wait and see," that so characterizes the modern use of *hope*.

Although the Bible speaks of men of hope being men of character, our society tends to mock men of hope, seeing them as dreamers and visionaries who are out of touch with reality. Our scientifically oriented society has difficulty in dealing with faith and hope, although all of our technology came about because others invested their lives in their hopes. Edison's multiple thousands of failures did not stop his experiments while he searched for a usable filament to transform electricity into light. He hoped against hope, and this favorable and confident expectation kept him moving from one substance to another until finally his hopes were fully realized in a workable incandescent lamp. He had visualized it as possible and pursued his hopes until it was virtual and practical.

The Position of Hope

In his concluding statement on the great apology of love, Paul defined "faith, hope, and love" as the three enduring pillars of the Christian confession (1 Corinthians 13:13 RSV). Again and again Paul united these three in his writings. In the introduction to his letter to the Thessalonians, he wrote, "Remembering without ceasing your work of *faith,* and labour of *love,* and patience of *hope* in our Lord Jesus Christ . . ." (1 Thessalonians 1:3, italics added). To the Church at Rome he wrote, "By whom also we have access by *faith* . . . and rejoice in *hope.* . . . And hope maketh not ashamed; because the *love* of God is shed abroad in our hearts by the Holy Ghost which is given unto us" (Romans 5:2–5, italics added); and, ". . . let us prophesy according to the proportion of *faith.* . . . Let *love* be without dissimulation. . . . Rejoicing in *hope* . . ." (Romans 12:6,9,12, italics added).

Here in the first chapter of Colossians we have the same triad: "Since we heard of your *faith* . . . and of the *love.* . . . For the *hope* . . ." (verses 4,5, italics added). The *New English Bible* translates this fifth verse, "Both spring from the hope stored up for you in heaven . . .," giving us a better understanding of this repeated triad. Faith and love both spring from hope. It is almost as though Paul visualized hope as a gushing fountain of pure water atop a tall mountain. Some of this water flowed down one side of the mountain, eventually forming a river of faith, while the rest of the water flowed down the opposite side of the mountain, forming a mighty stream of love, but although both streams flowed in different directions, each had its source in the same fountain. Hope is the fountainhead from which both faith and love flow. It is the quality from which faith springs and the atmosphere in which love grows. It is the Christian hope within us that fosters and ferments the faith and love which flow out of us.

The Nature of Hope

Hope is a firm expectation of all promised good things and is founded upon the promises of God. It deals with things future whereas faith is concerned with the present and love with the past, present, and future. Hope concerns itself with things as yet unseen, things not yet in our time dimension; it is a strong force that God has given to us whereby we can deal with an area that is not yet ours.

When hope is dashed upon the rocks of despair, love leaves and faith falters, for hopelessness is not an atmosphere in which faith and love can long survive. Recognizing this, Paul urges us "to lay hold upon the hope set before us: Which hope we have as an anchor of the soul, both sure and stedfast . . ." (Hebrews 6:18,19). Hope, then, is not only the fountainhead, or source, of our faith and love; it is also their foundation or security. What is begun in hope is bound up in that hope. That which started their flow secures that flow. Hope is the cradle and crucible of our faith and love, and the enemy must destroy that hope before he can demolish our faith toward God and our love of the brethren.

The Importance of Hope

The importance of hope is seen plainly in Hebrews 11:1: "Now faith is the substance [faith gives substance NEB] of things hoped for, the evidence of things not seen." Faith is declared the substance, the reality, of what began in hope. Faith and hope are not in opposition to each other; one flows out of the other and makes real what was once little more than an attitude or desire. Even here where "hope" is connected to "things" it does not say that "faith is the substance of things *believed* for," but "faith is the substance of things *hoped* for." Faith will give substance to those things we need if we have hope and if we keep hope alive. An exuberant, expectant attitude toward the promises of God will surely open us to a flow of the faith of God, and will contribute to our reception of those things for which we have hoped. Hope is, therefore, essential to the function of faith.

Hope affects our attitudes and actions; it gives boldness and authority; it revitalizes our emotions and even affects our body chemistry. Paul said, "Seeing then that we have such hope, we use great plainness [boldness] of speech" (2 Corinthians 3:12). Hope and boldness are inseparably linked.

Picture a ship mercilessly battered in a storm at sea. Exhaustedly the crew mans the pumps, lashes the cargo, and fulfills the captain's orders, while the radio man desperately calls for help. If the captain's report to the crew is, "We can't get a call through; it is hopeless!" the crew loses its courage and strength; they give up their exhausting efforts and await the inevitable. But if the message is, "We've gotten through to another ship nearby, and help is on its way!" new strength flows through the crew and their efforts are redoubled. Hope has given them new boldness, renewed strength, and fresh determination.

In my second pastorate, Dr. Ralph deBit, who delivered two of our children, occasionally phoned me to say, "Reverend, I have a patient in the hospital who needs you. He has given up. I can't help him any further unless he wants to live, and believes that he can. Will you visit him and see if you can rekindle fresh hope in him? Unless you do I'm afraid we'll have to bury him." Repeatedly, I found that hope was a better medicine than surgery, for until the patient hoped he could survive, the necessary inner forces needed to combat the workings of death would not function.

In my nearly thirty years of pastoring I repeatedly saw people whose lives were turned around by hope. Although I could not change their circumstances, and frequently could not inspire faith, if I could impart a real hope to them everything else began to fall into place. I have seen marriages rescued from the divorce courts by a little spark of hope, and have watched despondent men square their shoulders and face life one more time after a fresh hope has been inspired in them. I've seen students who failed in their first semester of college go on to graduate with honors primarily because someone infused hope into them in the midst of their failure. Hope is a force so great that it can turn our attitudes from negative to positive, redirect our faith from failure to success, and rekindle strength in the midst of extreme weakness. "We are saved by hope . . ." Paul wrote (Romans 8:24), where he used the Greek word *sozo* for "saved." This word encompasses a scope far greater than mere deliverance from sin and hell; it is concerned with the completeness of God's provision for that redeemed man from the cross of conversion to the crown of heavenly rewards. Hope is the flow of that deliverance and provision.

The Function of Hope

Hope concerns itself with the *Logos* of God, that which God has spoken, while faith involves the *Rhema*, that which God is speaking. While faith comes by action of the *Rhema* ("Faith cometh by hearing the Word of God" [*see* Romans 10:17]), hope comes by just looking at the *Logos*. As the things God has declared become alive to us, hope springs up within us because we are looking with the positive persuasion that what God has promised He is also able to perform.

As with Joshua, God oftens takes a man to the mountain and lets him see the wide expanse of promise and then says, *I'm going to let you have every place the sole of your feet treads* (*see* Joshua 1:3). The sight engenders hope and desire, which motivate that man into activity. As he moves in the stream of hope that flows deep within his spirit, faith comes alive and begins to function, and out of that faith comes possession of the territory covered in the promise of God.

When we see God's promises in their full spectrum, hope within us declares that what is now but a vision will someday become a reality. Having viewed the promise, there is hope that God's promise can come alive, and such an atmosphere makes hearing God far easier. When God speaks, of course, faith flows, and we function in believing. Hope and faith work together as surely as the *Logos* and the *Rhema* harmonize. Sometimes their differences are more theological than actual. One flows into the other with such gentleness that it is almost as difficult to draw a line of demarcation between them as it is to separate the actions of the spirit and the soul.

Thank God for hope; it is valuable and vital to our Christian life. Although it is not faith, it is a source of, and a channel for, our faith.

In his book *Eternal Hope* Emil Brunner says:

Hope nears the presence of the future, or more precisely, it is one of the ways in which what is merely future and potential is made vividly present and actual to us. Hope is the positive, as anxiety is the negative, mode of awaiting the future.

The Need for Hope

There is a desperate need for hope. Emil Brunner says:

What oxygen is for the lungs, such is the hope for the meaning of human life. Take oxygen away and death occurs through suffocation; take hope away and humanity is constricted through lack of breath; despair supervenes, spelling the paralysis of intellectual and spiritual powers by a feeling of senselessness and purposelessness of existence. As the fate of the human organism is dependent upon the supply of oxygen, so the fate of humanity is dependent upon its supply of hope.

Man needs hope because he is an eternal creature and cannot live long confined to the present. If he has accepted Christ, he has eternal life; otherwise, he has eternal death. Either way, he is a participant in eternity.

Eternity has no past, present, or future, as times does. As Christians, we have a life that always was and always will be. We are participants way back in the dealings of God with Abraham, and we are participants far ahead in the dealings of God in the heavenlies. At present, we can't understand this completely, but eternal life given to us at salvation through Christ starts in the beginning with God and flows right out into the eternities with God.

Since we Christians are now living in eternal life, actuated by eternal life, and motivated by eternal life, if all we deal with is the present, we become very miserable and dissatisfied people, for God has made us eternal creatures. There is within us now that which insists, desires, yearns, and is inspired to reach beyond the present into eternity, and God in His grace has given us hope to enable us to do so.

We cannot release faith into the future, for faith functions in our now, but we can have hope for the future. There is something beyond the veil of natural years, and God has graciously given us glowing promises about the hope that is laid up for us in heaven.

Until there is hope, it is most unlikely there will be faith. God not only gives us hope to enable us to deal with the future but He gives us hope to be able to deal with the present as well. Sometimes when we hear a message from the Word of God, or a Christian song with a message, a spark of hope is ignited within us. Then from that hope flows such expectation as to kindle the flame of faith. Something happens because a ray of hope was stirred within us.

Several years ago I accepted an invitation to spend a Sunday with a church that had enjoyed a good past, but due to a series of related circumstances things had gone from bad to worse. The congregation had declined numerically, finances were so small that payments on the property had fallen far behind the contract, and they had no pastor. The few remaining people were prepared to sell their building and disband themselves as a church. Despair was as thick as a London fog that day. I knew that I had just this one day to speak to these despondent ones, so I chose to extend them a hope in God's provision. During that day this spark of hope began to light a fire in their hearts and something happened. They chose not to sell and disband but to call a pastor and reach for a future as great as their past had been. Hope had channeled some faith in their hearts. It worked! For months they had far more hope than faith, but faith began to function, and I returned repeatedly to feed their hope.

During the years that have ensued this congregation has kept me informed of their progress. They have grown, paid off their mortgage, enlarged to where two morning services are now required, and they are making plans for a greatly enlarged building. It all started when God simply inspired a little hope so that they could step out of despair, back into a fearless looking at the promises of God, and from looking to believing, and from believing to receiving.

We must be careful not to condemn a person who is not functioning in faith and love. Instead, we should channel a flow of our hope, pour a little expectation on their pessimism, and share a bit of the desire that is ours. This will get their stream of hope flowing to give the thirsty a taste of hope's water, and soon faith and love will flow, and hope will again have been used as a fountainhead of life to the needy.

The more hopeless life seems to become, the more we need this flow of hope. These are difficult days of double-digit inflation, anarchy, terrorism, and international intrigue, and there is little basis for optimism as we peer into the future. Surely the prophetic words of Jesus are literally being fulfilled today: "Men's hearts failing them for fear, and for looking after those things which are coming on the earth . . ." (Luke 21:26). This should not be so with Christians, for "we have full assurance of hope unto the end" (*see* Hebrews 6:11).

Today's Church needs a fresh flow from the fountainhead of hope, from which renewed faith and love can flow, enabling us to stand in the hard times. Turbulence and tribulation should not affect our relationship with the Lord Jesus, with our brothers and sisters, or even with ourselves. God has given us a great measure of hope that becomes a preserving power in the midst of pressures. Even when faith seems to be exhausted, hope continues to flow, singing like a babbling brook, "Believe God! Believe God!"

We are not abandoned to our fate by an unfeeling and unapproachable God; instead, ". . . we . . . have a strong consolation, who have fled for refuge to lay hold upon the hope set before us: Which hope we have as an anchor of the soul, both sure and stedfast, and which entereth into that within the veil" (Hebrews 6:18, 19). As we lay hold upon hope there is consolation and comfort, and that hope reaches all the way through the veil of time into the Holy of Holies where God abides. Standing thus before the throne of grace we receive all the help we need to meet every crisis of daily living (Hebrews 4:16). God's help starts with our hope!

Even when sorrow comes, and it will come to the Christian, Paul tells us that our hope tempers that sorrow to such an extent that it is unlike the sorrow experienced by non-Christians. ". . . ye sorrow not, as others which have no hope," he wrote (1 Thessalonians 4:13). How much easier it is for a pastor to conduct the funeral of a believer than a nonbeliever, for although he must deal with the genuine sorrow at the loss of a loved one, he does not face the hopelessness and the sense of finality that characterizes the response at the interment of one who died without Christ. "Blessed be the God," Peter wrote, ". . . which according to his abundant mercy hath begotten us again unto a lively hope by the resurrection of Jesus Christ from the dead" (1 Peter 1:3).

Further Triads in Hope

So much of God's revelation to man is connected with threes. Our God is revealed as a Trinity, man is tripartite in nature, the approach to God as illustrated in the tabernacle involves three separate courts, and there are three eternal facets of our faith. Not only are faith, hope, and love connected as triads repeatedly in the New Testament but there are also other triads to be observed when tracing the New Testament's teaching on hope.

For instance, there are *three descriptive adjectives* associated with the word *hope* in the New Testament. It is called a "good hope" (2 Thessalonians 2:16), a "blessed hope" (Titus 2:13), and a "lively hope" (1 Peter 1:3). It is good because of its contribution to faith and love. It is blessed because its source is in God, who alone is blessed. It is lively because it rejuvenates dying mankind. The "good hope" enables man to function in good works. The "blessed hope" brings God's blessings into human behavior, and the "lively hope" brings eternal life into the temporal here and now. It is a good, blessed, and lively hope in that nothing on earth can remain good, blessed, or lively without it. Hope is the difference between good and bad, blessing and cursing, and living or dying in this life and the next.

There are also *three comparative nouns* related to hope in the New Testament. We read of the "helmet" of hope (1 Thessalonians 5:8), the "anchor" of hope (Hebrews 6:19), and the "assurance" of hope (Hebrews 6:11). As a "helmet," hope becomes part of the Christian's armor, and is equated with our salvation, since that is what the helmet is called in Paul's description of the entire Christian armor in Ephesians 6:13. There is no conflict in this, for the same writer declares, "We are saved by hope . . ." (Romans 8:24). As an "anchor," hope becomes our security amidst storms and the strength of our mooring in the harbor of rest, for it is declared, ". . . moreover also my flesh shall rest in hope" (Acts 2:26). As an "assurance," hope reaffirms God's promises, reminds us consistently of God's performance, and dispels doubts about our present perplexities. ". . . experience [worketh] hope: And hope maketh not ashamed . . ." (Romans 5:4,5). The assurance of hope brings the experience of the past and the expectation of the future into an expediency in the present. Hope challenges us to "continue . . . in the things which thou hast learned and hast been assured of . . ." (2 Timothy 3:14). Our minds are protected by the "helmet" of hope; our lives are secured by the "anchor" of hope; and our hearts are comforted through the "assurance of hope."

Furthermore, there are *three possessive pronouns* linked to hope. It is named "my hope" (Psalms 39:7), "your hope" (1 Peter 1:21), and "our hope" (1 Timothy 1:1). Hope is personal, individual, and collective. It may begin in an individual, find strength in fellowship with another believer, and find expression in the body of believers. Conversely, it may first find expression in Christ's Church, be exemplified in the life of a close associate, and then begin to spring up in the individual's life. But whatever the order of reception or expression, it is never declared "God's hope"; it is always "our," "your," or "my" hope. God may be the Source and Object of that hope, but we are the recipients, the channels, and the beneficiaries of hope, so it is our hope. It is a personal possession, my, your hope; it is a participating possession, our hope; and it is a present possession since it is already declared to belong to me and you.

In the original manuscripts of the New Testaments there are *three Greek prepositions* combined with hope: *eis,* as in ". . . who hoped *in* God . . ." (1 Peter 3:5 RSV, italics added) directing our attention to the truth that hope centers in a person; *epi,* ". . . *in* him shall the Gentiles hope" (Romans 15:12 RSV, italics added) expressing the ground upon which hope rests; and *en* as, ". . . we have hoped *in* Christ . . ." (1 Corinthians 15:19 RSV, italics added), which W. E. Vine declares in his book *Expository Dictionary of New Testament Words:*

> . . . literally means "We are (men) that have hoped in Christ," the preposition expresses that Christ is not simply the ground upon whom, but the sphere and element in whom, the hope is placed. The form of the verb (the perfect participle with the verb to be, lit. "are having hoped") stresses the character of those who hope, more than the action; hope characterizes them, showing what sort of persons they are.

Still a fourth triad of terms connected with hope might be the *English verbs* used with hope. Looking toward the glorious appearing of our Lord and Saviour, Jesus Christ, John wrote, "Every man that hath this hope in him *purifieth* himself, even as he is pure" (1 John 3:3, italics added). Hope is a cleansing force in the life of the Christian. Because of our hope in and of Christ we will decontaminate, chasten, and purge ourselves of sin, selfishness, and satanic influence. Our sanctification is motivated far more by our hope in God's promises than in our fear of God's punishments. We desire purity because of our hope in Christ.

Hope purifies, but hope also abounds. The context surrounding this statement is forceful: "Now the God of hope fill you with all joy and peace in believing, that ye may *abound* in hope, through the power of the Holy Ghost" (Romans 15:13, italics added). God initially fills the believer with joy and peace (two of the earliest fruit of the Spirit to mature, according to Galatians 5:22) in order that we may "abound in hope." There is no shortage of joy, peace, or hope, for God's gift is more than ample. No Christian should try to subsist on a miniscule quantity of hope when God has made it available in teeming prevalency. We should have a sufficiency of hope; it should multiply within us, and there should be innumerable things for which we hope in Christ. Our hope abounds!

Furthermore, our hope *rejoices!* "Rejoicing in hope . . ." Paul declares (Roman 12:12). Hope's expression is never pessimistic; it is always positive and praise filled. A person filled with hope is automatically a person filled with praise. The person bubbling with reassurance is also effervescent with rejoicing. It is he who can exult greatly in the Lord. It is the hope-filled Christian who delights himself in God and His ways, and finds happiness in this life commensurate with his hope in the life to come. How can one be filled with hope in Christ and not be a rejoicing Christian when the very Greek noun *elpis* most frequently signifies "the happy anticipation of good." Hopeful Christians are happy Christians.

Three Statements About Hope in Colossians 1

Hope is *preserved,* laid up, for us in heaven according to verse 5. This wonderful hope, without which man does not live—he only exists—is on deposit in God's eternal heaven. It's available for use as needed. Since we know that "If in this life only we have hope in Christ, we are of all men most miserable" (1 Corinthians 15:19), God, in His goodness, has laid up a hope for us in the eternities so that not only in this life but in that life which is yet to come there's a hope preserved for us, a treasured hope protected for us.

God's goal for us is not merely that we'll get so much better that we'll enjoy things here on earth, but He is preparing us to live in His presence for all eternity. This hope of a new world awaiting us keeps the saints in a state of purification, actuation, and motivation. It is comforting to know that we do not have to preserve our hope; He is doing it for us!

Hope is *presented* to us on earth according to verse 23: "If ye . . . be not moved away from the hope of the gospel, which ye have heard, and which was preached to every creature which is under heaven; whereof I Paul am made a minister." Similarly, Paul said to "lay hold upon the hope set before us" (Hebrews 6:18). We do not await hope's arrival; it has come! The message of hope has been presented to every creature under heaven; it has been presented to men ever since the angel who announced the birth of Jesus declared to the shepherds, "Fear not: for, behold, I bring you good tidings of great joy, which shall be to all people" (Luke 2:10). We are not asked to produce hope, only to receive it; it is one of God's gifts to men. It is not something that needs as much to be sought as it needs to be caught. It has been provided for us. Life starts anew for us when we kneel at the cross and by a simple act of faith invite Jesus Christ to live in us and be Lord over us. Only the Gospel hope can make a man, woman, boy, or girl live again. This hope was presented to a lost world when Jesus came as the Saviour.

This hope is *personalized* in Jesus according to verse 27: ". . . Christ in you, the hope of glory." That God is the Author of all of our hopes is not contested, for the Scriptures clearly define Him as, "the God of hope" (Romans 15:13). He is the Source of all our hope; without Him life would be meaningless, and the future would be hopeless. God, through Christ, is the Source of all the believer's expectations. Paul reminded Timothy of this when he wrote, ". . . Lord Jesus Christ, which is our hope" (1 Timothy 1:1). Even the Old Testament Psalmist knew this, for he sang, ". . . my hope is in thee" (Psalms 39:7), and "Happy is he . . . whose hope is in the Lord his God" (Psalms 146:5).

Jesus is God's hope for mankind. Christ in us is the Source of all our hope. When our hope is exhausted we can still draw upon the hope of the Christ who lives within us. Of the godly patriarch Abraham, the Word says, "Who against hope believed in hope . . ." (Romans 4:18). Moffat's translation reads, ". . . when all hope was gone, he hoped on in faith. . . ." This aging man exhausted all his hopes for a son, even after the promise of God came to him, but he had learned a resource from which he could renew his hopes. He reviewed the promise God had made to him; God's Word was a reservoir of hope for him. We New Testament saints have an advantage over Abraham, for "The Word was made flesh, and dwelt among us . . ." (John 1:14); for us it is, "Christ in you, the hope . . ." (Colossians 1:27).

Christ's sacramental cross and His Second Coming form the taproot for our hope. Jesus is the Source of our hope. He is the Object of our hope. He has become God's supply line of hope to the believers. All the good promises of God find their fulfillment in Christ Jesus. His life within us, by means of the Holy Spirit, is a constant source of the renewal of our hope. As surely as "In him we live, and move, and have our being . . ." (Acts 17:28), in Christ we trust, hope, and have our expectation. He is our Hope!

7

Jesus, Our Deliverer

"Who hath delivered us from the power of darkness . . ." (Colossians 1:13).

Jesus Christ is not only our Hope—our joyful expectation of the future and our confident anticipation of good—He is our Deliverer! He "hath delivered us from . . ." Paul declares (Colossians 1:13).

While I am fully aware that the "who" of verse thirteen refers directly to the "Father" of verse twelve, the New Testament teaches us that God the Father provided our deliverance, God the Son produced that deliverance, God the Spirit presents it to men, and we participate in it. God begat our deliverance; we are merely its beneficiaries. He engineered it; we just enjoy it.

We were not assisted in gaining a deliverance; He delivered us as surely as Israel was delivered from Egypt by the divine intervention of a covenant-keeping God. For Israel, Moses was the deliverer. He pronounced the plagues upon the enemy, led the people out of bondage, opened the Red Sea, and led them to the Promised Land, but for us, Jesus Christ is the Deliverer. It is He who spoiled the enemy, led us out of the bondage of sin, united us into the body of believers by baptism, and is safely conducting us to a Promised Land in His heaven.

Because "Jesus Christ [is] the same yesterday, and to day, and for ever" (Hebrews 13:8), our deliverance not only touches the past but it reaches into eternity as well. Paul told the Corinthians, "Who *delivered* us from so great a death, and *doth deliver:* in whom we trust that He *will yet deliver* us" (2 Corinthians 1:10, italics added).

The act of delivering us is in the past, while the fact of our deliverance remains active in the present, and this pact of deliverance will continue valid through all eternity.

Jesus Divided the Darkness

The enslaving force from which Christ has delivered us is called "the power of darkness" by Paul (Colossians 1:13). Other translators render the word *power* variously. Rotherham interprets the Greek word as "authority" and writes, "Who hath rescued us out of the *authority* of the darkness." Conybeare expresses it, ". . . from the *dominion* of the darkness." Verkuyl says, ". . . from the *control* of darkness," while the *Living Bible* reads, ". . . out of the darkness and *gloom* of Satan's kingdom . . ." (all italics added).

Jesus has delivered us from far more than mere sin. He has rescued us from the authority, dominion, control, and gloom of Satan's kingdom, for Satan is "the ruler of the darkness of this world" (*see* Ephesians 6:12), his kingdom is filled with darkness (Revelation 16:10), and his habitation is called "chains of darkness" (2 Peter 2:4). By parable, Jesus taught that those expelled into this "other kingdom" were expelled into "outer darkness" (Matthew 8:12; 22:13; 25:30), and at His arrest and trial Christ spoke of the force behind it all as "the power of darkness" (Luke 22:53).

Consistently through the Scriptures we see two separate, distinct, opposing kingdoms: the Kingdom of God and the kingdom of the devil. Although they are far from equal, and the leader of the kingdom of darkness was created by the leader of the Kingdom of light, the two kingdoms are competitive in exercising authority over mankind, and each is an antithesis to the other. The lives of the subjects of these kingdoms will be as opposite as the kingdoms themselves. Satan enslaves and oppresses, while Jesus grants men their free moral agency. The kingdom of darkness blinds men, while the Kingdom of light illuminates them.

The work of Christ's deliverance is to bring us out of darkness into His Kingdom of light. He is not content merely to erase a few actions and change a few attitudes; His work is to translate us out of one kingdom into the other, "and hath translated us into the kingdom of His dear Son" (Colossians 1:13). In giving his testimony to King Agrippa, Paul said that his commission was "To open their eyes, and to turn them from darkness to light, and from the power of Satan unto God . . ." (Acts 26:18). Peter also recognized the nature of Christ Jesus' redemptive work when he urged us to "shew forth the praises of him who hath called you out of darkness into his marvellous light" (1 Peter 2:9). Like Israel under Moses, we are being brought *out of* one kingdom *into* another.

Jesus asked the Pharisees, "How can one enter into a strong man's house, and spoil his goods, except he first bind the strong man? and then he will spoil his house" (Matthew 12:29). Christ knew that He had to break the power and authority of Satan before He could deliver any of us from the satanic kingdom.

Jesus Disintegrated Satan's Works

Furthermore, He did just that! John, the beloved, testified, ". . . For this purpose the Son of God was manifested, that He might destroy the works of the devil" (1 John 3:8). The Greek word he chose to use for "destroy" is *luō,* which basically means "to come unglued, to loose, or cause to lose consistency."

This loosing of *luō* is like when mortar becomes rotten and crumbles so that a brick building slowly disintegrates. It is like a beautifully handcrafted table whose joints slip apart because the glue used in its construction has decomposed and lost its adhesive powers. It is like a woman's sewing if the bobbin runs out of thread. All of the pieces remain, but they lack any cohesive force to keep them together.

God chose this method instead of a frontal assault against the satanic kingdom because it is not yet time for Satan's complete downfall. Although the conflict between these two kingdoms is multiplied thousands of years old, it has never been a direct war between God and Lucifer. For now, God is content to let His archangel Michael use heaven's lesser angels to confront Lucifer and his angels. It is not yet a battle to conquer; it is more like an occupational army sent to control. When God does enter the battle with Satan it will end all of the devil's activity and leave him banished into the lake of fire forever and forever.

The specific work of our lovely Jesus was not to destroy the devil, but to "destroy the works of the devil" (1 John 3:8), to make everything he had built crumble and break down, and He did it magnificently! He accomplished His mission by being the opposite of everything Satan is declared to be.

Works of Darkness Illuminated

We've already seen the extreme contrast between the kingdoms of God and Satan: they are light and darkness. Imagine the confusion and frustration it must have caused this former angel of light, who, upon his expulsion from heaven, lost his Source of light and was consigned to a kingdom of darkness, when Jesus came demonstrating and declaring, "I am the light of the world" (John 8:12). All the evil works of darkness were immediately exposed. Satan's "hidden things of darkness" (1 Corinthians 4:5) were instantly unveiled under the spotlight of God's Son. Like insects scurrying for darkness when a board is turned over, the devil's henchmen fled from this light. Even before Christ spoke a word, demons cried out, "What have we to do with thee, Jesus, thou Son of God? . . ." (Matthew 8:29). Light will always cause a kingdom of darkness to disintegrate, for there is no power in darkness; it is merely the absence of light. ". . . he that followeth me," Jesus said, "shall not walk in darkness, but shall have the light of life" (John 8:12). From His first appearance, Jesus caused the dark walls of Satan's kingdom to begin to crumble.

Works of Deceit Revealed

Similarly, the devil, who is a known deceiver, holds his kingdom together by deception. He tempts men through the "deceitfulness of riches" (Matthew 13:22), lures them by "the deceitful lusts" of their human nature (Ephesians 4:22), and confuses even the righteous with "false apostles [and] deceitful workers" (2 Corinthians

11:13). Jesus warned that the capacity of the devil and his kingdom to deceive is so great that "if it were possible, they shall deceive the very elect" (Matthew 24:24). If it hadn't been for Jesus, most, if not all, of us would be hopelessly deceived, for even education is no security against demonic deception; just look at the success of some of the cults in our enlightened society.

When Jesus stepped into this kingdom of deception He began to make revelations. He amazed His disciples by telling Nathanael, "I saw you under the fig tree" upon their very first meeting (*see* John 1:48), and He completely convinced the woman at the well of His Messiahship by merely revealing her marital status (John 4). He revealed the unbiblical tradition of the religion of the Jews (Mark 7:7,8). He exposed the secrets of men's hearts, and He revealed the Heavenly Father to mankind. Such constant revelations rotted the glue of the devil's kingdom and it began to fall apart, very much as indoor plywood falls apart in the rain because it is not made with waterproof adhesive.

Works of Lies Unveiled

Harmonious with his deception, Satan is an incurable liar, and the variegated pieces of his kingdom are sewn together with lies. He is a liar both by title and by nature. His first communication with man was a lie: "Ye shall not surely die" (Genesis 3:4), and every subsequent communication has been a lie. He is not capable of telling more than a half-truth, which is the most dangerous form of a lie there is. In speaking of Satan, Jesus told His disciples: ". . . When he speaketh a lie, he speaketh of his own: for he is a liar, and the father of it" (John 8:44).

Mark Twain reportedly said, "The problem of being a liar is that it requires a fabulous memory." But this would be no problem for Satan, for he possesses both a supernatural memory and an uncanny ability to lie. After all, he is the father of liars. He built a great kingdom on lies, promising men things that he never intended to do. His lies cause persons to destroy their minds and bodies by the use of drugs, alcohol, and tobacco. His lies break up homes, destroy friendships, and foment wars. He lies to men about

God, to God about men, and to people about people, and he makes his lies very believable.

Nevertheless, when Jesus bridged the gap between heaven and earth, "The Word was made flesh, and dwelt among us . . . *full of grace and truth*" (John 1:14, italics added). When He entered into His ministry right in the midst of Satan's kingdom of lies, Jesus said, "I am the . . . truth . . ." (John 14:6). From that moment on it was the beginning of the end for the devil's deceitful kingdom of lies, for no lie retains its power of control once the truth is fully revealed, since truth causes lies to fall apart as much as the removal of the bobbin thread ruins the stitches of the seamstress. Satan's kingdom could not hold together where the truth of God was revealed, for the locking stitch was missing, and the several parts disconnected and fell apart. By simply being "the truth," Jesus destroyed (*luō*) the works of the devil.

Works of Murderer Resurrected

Furthermore, Satan is a murderer who holds much of his kingdom together through the threat of death. From the day he succeeded in getting Adam to trade access to the Tree of Life for access to the Tree of Knowledge, he has pursued his murderous trade both as a fulfillment of his inner hatred and as intimidation to gain control of men. It was very evident in his murdering all children in Bethlehem two years old and under at the time of the birth of Jesus as he zealously sought to assassinate the Christ in His infancy. This killing instinct of Satan is further revealed in the countless deaths of the martyrs, in the so-called holy wars and Crusades, and more recently in the tragic suicide-murder of the entire colony of the Jim Jones cult in Guyana, South America. Besides these mass-murderous acts, only God knows what percentage of the daily suicides and murders in the world are demonically inspired, but we may surmise that it is a very large percentage. Jesus told the scribes and Pharisees, "Ye are of your father the devil, and the lusts of your father ye will do. He was a murderer from the beginning . . ." (John 8:44).

As surely as the underworld weaves the fabric of its extortion and control over countless businessmen through threats of violent death and destruction, so Satan has intimidated people of all generations to do his will. He threatens sickness, disease, and death to motivate men.

Yet when Jesus came, He "went about doing good, and healing all that were oppressed of the devil; for God was with him (Acts 10:38). The resurrection of Jairus's daughter (Mark 5:35–42), the interruption of the funeral procession at Nain as Jesus raised the man out of the casket and restored him to his widowed mother (Luke 7:11–15), and the calling forth of Lazarus after he had been entombed at least three days (John 11) took the teeth out of Satan's weapon of death, for Christ could restore the dead to life again.

In the simplicity of Christ's coming He repeatedly demonstrated that He could easily undo anything that Satan had done or could do. By Christ's illumination, revelation, and Resurrection, Satan's kingdom began falling apart at the seams as his works were systematically destroyed (*luō*) by the presence of Jesus. This disintegrating of the satanic kingdom is still taking place, because Jesus is alive forevermore, continuing to do through His body, the Church, what He did while in the earthly body God prepared for Him through Mary.

Even today the mortar in the devil's stone walls rots and crumbles and the cohesive force that holds his unwieldy kingdom together loses its binding power, causing everything to come unglued, when Christians demonstrate the life of Jesus Christ on earth, for how long can hatred remain in the presence of love? What power does darkness have when light has come? What control can a lie exert in the presence of the truth? How long can the threat of death intimidate in the face of resurrection life being demonstrated in the Church?

As the antithesis of this, the same divine energy that causes Satan's kingdom to come unglued is binding Christ's Kingdom into a working force of increasing strength, for the Spirit of God functioning in the Church today is forming strong bonds of unity, faith, and love. Just as "David waxed stronger and stronger, and the house of Saul waxed weaker and weaker" (2 Samuel 3:1), so the

Church on earth is enlarging and gaining spiritual strength through the very same processes that are weakening and crumbling Satan's kingdom. The Church can joyfully quote Solomon: "The way of the Lord is strength to the upright: but destruction shall be to the workers of iniquity" (Proverbs 10:29).

Jesus Denied Satan the Power of Death

In breaking Satan's power and authority over us so that we could be delivered from his dominion and his domain, Jesus not only caused the devil's works to be decimated, exposed, and destroyed (*luō*) but He also annulled, obliterated, and invalidated Satan's most formidable weapon—the power of death. It is no longer a case of Christ's undoing the effects of death through resurrection, but the power to produce death in the first place was snatched away from Satan by Jesus.

The writer to the Hebrews describes this kind of destruction:

> Forasmuch then as the children are partakers of flesh and blood, he also himself likewise took part of the same; that through death he might destroy him that had the power of death, that is, the devil; And deliver them who through fear of death were all their lifetime subject to bondage.
>
> Hebrews 2:14,15

Jesus came to destroy him who *had* (past tense) the power of death. The Greek word Paul elected to use for "destroy" is *katargeō*, which means "to make of no effect, to render powerless, to reduce to a zero." By becoming man, who alone of God's higher order of creation is subject to death, and by His obedience in actually tasting death for all men, Jesus reduced to a zero Satan's ultimate power over the saints—the power of death—and furthermore, at His Ascension Jesus knocked the rim off that zero!

"Death hath no terrors for the blood-bought one, O glory hallelujah to the lamb!" we used to sing in my boyhood days. We who have been crucified with Christ and resurrected in Him to a newness of life need have no fear of death, for we can die only once, and we died in Christ Jesus. Death is a past, not a future, experience for the truly born-again one. It is not that our earthly bodies will not decay and dissolve back into the earth from whence they originally came, for "it is appointed unto men once to die . . ." (Hebrews 9:27), but when a saint is released from his earthly body he is immediately promoted to a higher spiritual plane. "We are confident," Paul wrote, "and willing rather to be absent from the body, and to be present with the Lord" (2 Corinthians 5:8). It is not death; it is graduation, and even that moment is no longer in Satan's power; Jesus promotes His own in His perfect time.

In the annals of warfare no major defeat has escaped the close scrutiny of hindsight to see just what battle turned the tide against the defeated one. In analyzing Satan's tactics, most historians agree that Calvary was his greatest error. Hell thought it had won a great victory when heaven's crowned prince was cruelly impaled on the rough Roman cross, but this was not only the turning of the tide; it was the beginning of the end for the entire satanic kingdom. What may have appeared on the surface to be a defeat for Jesus very shortly proved to be an ignominious defeat for Satan, for while the body of Jesus lay embalmed in Joseph's tomb, this Lord that Satan thought he had killed appeared in the midst of the abode of the dead preaching the Gospel of deliverance (1 Peter 3:19).

After three days, the voice of the Father echoed through the corridors of hell, *Jesus, come forth!*

Stepping up to Satan's office, Jesus said, "You heard the Father; give Me the keys!"

"I'll have someone let You out," Satan replied in a very grudging manner.

"Never mind," Jesus replied; "I'll be happy to let Myself out."

Picking up a large ring of master keys, Satan slowly fingered through the individual keys, searching for the one that would release Jesus from the control of death.

"Never mind looking for My key," Jesus said; "just give Me all of them." Snatching the keys from Satan's grasp, Jesus not only came forth in resurrection but He also released many others who had been dead for longer periods than He had. These resurrected saints went into the city of Jerusalem as startling proof that Jesus had gained permanent control over death and the grave (Matthew 27:52,53).

From His ascended position at the throne in heaven Jesus testified, "I am he that liveth, and was dead; and, behold, I am alive forevermore, Amen; and have the keys of hell and of death" (Revelation 1:18). The Greek word for "keys" is definitely plural. Jesus now possesses all the keys of death, hell, and the grave. He, not Satan, is in control.

The plan of the Father was that "through death [of Jesus] he might destroy [reduce to a zero] him that *had* the power of death, that is, the devil; And deliver them who through fear of death were all their lifetime subject to bondage" (Hebrews 2:14,15, italics added).

It's a tragedy to be so afraid of dying that we can't live, and yet this death phobia limits the lives of countless people, even Christians. I've known ministries that have not been released to the world because the minister had a terrorizing fear of flying.

When God began to release me to the nations of the world, I found myself to be apprehensive about functioning in other cultures, but God quickly proved Himself to be in charge of my life. I've known what it is to stand at attention with a rifle in my back in Zaire, to be dragged by my necktie through an angry mob of shouting Africans in Tanzania, and to be held by one person while another menacingly put a fist under my nose threatening to beat me up in Kenya, but I have been spared the fear that they could kill me. My life is "hid with Christ in God" (Colossians 3:3), and Satan cannot take my life from me.

Every time there is a plane crash I am asked if I don't fear that it might happen to me inasmuch as I travel close to one hundred thousand miles a year in commercial airlines. "Of course not," is my answer. Such fear would limit my ministry, hamper my travel, and terrorize my spirit. While I have no assurance that I won't die in a plane crash or through the mob action of opponents to the Gospel I preach, I do have abundant assurance that it cannot happen out of the will or timing of God.

I find it gloriously comforting to hear death's keys rattling in

Jesus' hand when I minister in various nations of the world. I may be in Satan's territory, surrounded by demonic activity, but I am untouchable, because Christ now possesses the keys which not only let us out of the grave but which let us into it as well. Because Jesus holds those keys, Satan has no power to cut off our lives, our ministries, or our victories.

The absolute reduction to a zero of Satan's power to kill a child of God was graphically demonstrated to me a few years ago in Australia. In the midst of my preaching on this very subject there was a loud crying out that was quite obviously demonic. The person through which this scream had been uttered was quickly ushered out of the auditorium.

After the service I was taken to the pastor's study and was asked if I could minister deliverance to this little lady. In response to my question, I was informed that she was a recent convert who had come out of deep sin. She was seated to the side of the pastor's desk facing him and looking more like a teenager than the mother of three children. Her smile was disarming and everything about her behavior was gentle, gracious, and composed.

I was still standing with my back to the door completely across the room from them. "I don't sense any demonic activity in her just now," I said, "but if whatever spirit moved upon her in the service is still present I'll just lay my hands on her and cast it out in the name of Jesus."

Almost instantly this demon cried out through her in a very masculine-sounding voice, "Don't touch her; she's mine! If you lay your hands on her I'll kill her!"

Ignoring this warning, I stretched out my hand and took a step toward the little woman, who had now lost all outer calm and composure. "Please stay away," she cried. "He'll really kill me."

"He can't kill you," I assured her; "he's a lying demon who no longer has the power of death."

At the pastor's urging I retreated to my original position at the door and listened as this new sister in the Lord explained how this evil spirit had controlled her actions since girlhood with this very same threat. He (or it) had manifested extreme jealousy over her and had driven her to repeated acts of immorality, trying to break up her marriage. This very night her husband had informed her that she would have divorce papers served on her in the morning, and that he wouldn't be home when she returned from church.

"Susan [a fictitious name]," I said, "you are being terrorized by a lie. Since you have received Jesus as your Saviour, Satan no longer has the power of life and death over you."

Insolently, the demon interrupted me and in a surly voice shouted, "Yes, I do have the power of death over Susan, and I warn you that if you touch her I'll kill her."

This produced quite a demonstration of fear in Susan, and the pastor again cautioned me to be careful of my actions.

"Are you certain she has been born again?" I asked him.

"Positive," he replied.

"Then the demon is bluffing. He has no right to remain in Susan now that she has given her spirit to God," I said.

Turning from the pastor and facing Susan squarely in the face, although I was still across the room, I said, "Demon, I'm going to call your bluff. God's Word says that Jesus took the keys of death away from your master. You can't kill Susan."

"Yes I can, and will, if you take one step toward us," the demon replied.

"How long will it take you to kill her?" I asked.

"Well," he said, and then paused. "I don't know—right away, I guess."

"Could you do it in a minute?" I asked.

"Of course!" he replied.

"All right, then, I'll give you exactly one minute to show us that you can kill her," I said. Turning the face of my watch so that I could more easily see the sweep second hand, I waited until it was at the twelve o'clock position and said, "You have exactly one minute from right now. Kill her if you can."

The pastor looked terrified and Susan began to cry, "No, no, I don't want to die."

Later, when I got back to my room, I marveled at my courage and daring, but when one is ministering under the unction of the Holy Spirit he is as bold as a lion.

Every fifteen seconds I told the demon how much time he had left.

Susan choked, gasped, cried out, and flailed her arms and legs so severely that when the pastor tried to restrain her physically he was badly bruised. That small girl of a woman seemed to have the strength of a wrestler.

I counted down the last ten seconds as dramatically as I knew how and at exactly sixty seconds said, "Time's up, demon. Stop!" Susan calmed down instantly.

"Why didn't you kill her?" I asked the demon.

"You didn't give me enough time," he replied.

"But you said you could do it in a minute," I taunted.

"I know, but I was mistaken. I need more time," he said pleadingly.

"I don't understand you," I said. "You claim such supernatural powers, and yet you couldn't kill this little woman. Either of us men could have killed her with our bare hands in less than a minute."

"Give me another minute," he pleaded, "just one more minute. I'll show you I still have the power to kill Susan."

"All right," I said. "You have an additional minute, starting right now."

There was a partial repeat of outward manifestation for about thirty seconds, and then complete inactivity. Slowly a smile came over Susan's face as the truth of God became real to her spirit. He couldn't do it!

At the end of sixty seconds I demanded, "Demon, why is Susan still alive and unharmed?"

"I can't do it; I can't do it," he sobbed, like a little boy.

I walked across the room toward Susan, telling her that I would now cast that demon out of her life forever.

"Wait a minute," she said. "Now that I know he does not have any power over me I would like to cast him out." She began praying the sweetest prayer of thanksgiving to God for His great deliverance from the power of Satan's kingdom, and then she very authoritatively commanded that spirit force to get out of her life forever.

It was several weeks before I learned the sequel to this incident. I had returned to this church and was told by the pastor that one of the ladies wanted me to meet her husband. It was Susan. It seems that when she returned home after casting out the demon, she had found her husband so engrossed in a television program that he hadn't left the house. Quietly removing her coat, she had slipped to his side and gently lowered herself into his lap and laid her head on his shoulder.

Almost instantly he stiffened and said, "What has happened to you? You're different from the woman who left the house earlier this evening."

She told him everything that had happened in the pastor's study. He admitted that he didn't understand it but certainly recognized that something had transpired.

After a few days he told Susan, "I would like to meet the man who delivered you."

As Susan introduced her husband to me she said, "This is the man who brought me my deliverance."

Immediately he began to express his appreciation to me and said their marriage was now better than ever.

"There must be some mistake," I said. "I am not the man who delivered Susan; Jesus did. May I introduce you to Him?"

Paul must have experienced this tremendous control of a death threat, for he wrote, "O wretched man that I am! who shall deliver me from the body of this death? I thank God through Jesus Christ our Lord ..." (Romans 7:24,25). Jesus is our Deliverer from the power of death. He destroyed (*katargeō*) Satan's right to kill.

Jesus Divested Satan of All Authority

There was still a third front in God's conflict with Satan in the skirmish to break the devil's power and authority over our lives so we could be translated out of the kingdom of darkness into God's Kingdom. Paul speaks of it in these terms: "And having spoiled principalities and powers, he made a shew of them openly, triumphing over them in it" (Colossians 2:15).

The Greek word we have translated as "spoiled" is *apekduomai*, which literally means "to divest wholly; to despoil." It is a military term that is used nowhere else in the New Testament, but Paul chose this word with full knowledge of its meaning and implication, for being raised a tentmaker whose output probably went to the vast Roman army, Paul was very likely familiar with both military procedure and vocabulary.

When a Roman general finally conquered his foe, especially if the battle had been long and especially hard fought, the official surrender often became a formal, full-dress affair with the two leaders facing each other in the presence of their respective armies. After the signing of such documents of surrender as might have been drawn up, the conqueror stepped up to the defeated general, who stood at rigid attention in his full-dress military uniform with all insignias, medals, badges, and other symbols of position and authority that pertained to his position of leadership. Systematically, the conqueror stripped these symbols off the uniform of the defeated general to the accompaniment of beating drums. When every symbol of power, authority, rank, and honor had been forcibly ripped from the uniform, the Roman general would announce, "Now all of these are mine by right of conquest. What you were, I now am. The titles you held, I now hold. Your armies will now obey me, and your nation will forever be subject to the rule of Rome."

This ritual was called *apekduomai*. Movie goers and TV viewers will recognize the ceremony from western scenes in which an officer of the cavalry was disgracefully stripped of his rank and drummed out of the service.

It was with full understanding of this ceremony that Paul declared that at the time of Christ's Ascension He divested Satan of every position of authority and every vestige of power that God had ever given him before the expulsion from heaven.

What a scene that must have been! Jesus, pausing in His Ascension through the satanic kingdom to call for a full-dress parade, demanded that Satan stand at attention in full-dress uniform. Jesus stepped before him and in a voice that rang clear into the corridors of hell, declared, "Now is come salvation, and strength, and the kingdom of our God, and the power of his Christ: for the accuser of our brethren is cast down, which accused them before our God day and night" (Revelation 12:10). Reaching to the right epaulet of Satan's uniform, Jesus stripped it off, saying, "You were created Lucifer, which means 'day star' (Isaiah 14:12). I strip that title from you forever, for I shall be known as 'the bright and morning star'" (Revelation 22:16). Transferring this to His left hand, Jesus reached for the left epaulet and jerked it off the uniform, saying, "You held the position of the 'anointed cherub' (Ezekiel 28:14); but I now have the title of the 'Anointed One'" (*see* Acts 10:38).

Turning to His attending angel, Jesus directed that these epaulets be placed on the display table in full sight of the entire forces of hell.

Fixing His fingers on the gold braid of Satan's uniform, Jesus stripped it off in one quick action and said, "You have functioned as the 'tempter' (*see* Mark 1:13), but from now on I will be a 'guide' (Isaiah 58:11) to mankind."

Focusing His attention on the many medals Satan wore, Jesus began to strip them off the uniform one by one, authoritatively declaring, "I saw you as lightning falling (*see* Luke 10:18), but men shall see Me as lightning that shineth from the east to the west (*see* Matthew 24:27). You were the first creature of God's creation in which music was expressed (Ezekiel 28:13), but from now on '. . . in the midst of the church will I sing praise' (Hebrews 2:12). You have been an effective 'hinderer' (*see* 1 Thessalonians 2:18), but I will be a 'helper' (*see* Psalms 63:7). You have been that 'old serpent' (Revelation 12:9; 20:2), but I am as the serpent that was lifted up for men's healing (John 3:14). You have been an 'adversary' to My people (1 Peter 5:8), but I'm now their 'advocate' (1 John 2:1). You have functioned as an 'angel of light' (2 Corinthians 11:14), but 'I am the light of the world' (John 8:12). You have been the 'accuser of the brethren' (*see* Revelation 12:10), but I am now their 'Counseller' (Isaiah 9:6)."

With this, Jesus paused to place all these stripped medals into the care of the angel, who spread them out on the table to the side of Satan and Jesus. Both the armies of heaven and hell watched as Jesus reached for the five stars on the uniform of Satan. "I hereby strip you of your title of 'prince of this world' (John 14:30) and declare that I am both a 'Prince and a Saviour' (Acts 5:31); I am the 'Prince of Life' (Acts 3:15), and I am the 'KING OF KINGS AND LORD OF LORDS.' " (Revelation 19:16).

At this declaration the armies of heaven could restrain themselves no longer. In an excited cadence they cried, "Alleluia; Salvation, and glory, and honour, and power, unto the Lord our God: For true and righteous are his judgments ..." (Revelation 19:1,2).

Waiting for this demonstration to end, Jesus looked Satan coldly in the eyes and, without blinking an eyelid, reached for the stars on the other collar, declaring amidst His icy stare, "You were created as one of the sons of God (Job 1:6), but I am *'The* Son of God' (Mark 1:1; John 1:18, italics added). You have lost everything my Father gave to you; they are now My possessions."

Stripped, humiliated, and divested of all authority, Satan had to remain at attention while Jesus lifted these various symbols of position and rank in full sight of hell's armies. In the relieved voice of a conqueror, Jesus told them, "Satan and his entire kingdom are defeated. All of his power has been stripped from him. His authority has been transferred back to Me, and his kingdoms are now My kingdoms. You will henceforth be under the rule of the Heavenly Kingdom. Bounds and limits will be set upon your activities beyond which you will not dare to go. Failure to comply means you will have to deal with Me. I am your God, and you will obey Me."

At the sound of this proclamation the anger, frustration, and incredulity that had characterized the attitude of hell's legions gave way to fear. They cowed, turned their heads, trembled, and some even collapsed in their ranks. There was no doubt in any mind that Jesus Christ had fully conquered them once and for all.

Gathering all of these tattered remnants of Satan's power and authority, Jesus completed His Ascension into the heavens where He put them in a display case for all of heaven's inhabitants to see. Every angel in the eternal abodes knows that Satan has been completely stripped—*apekduomai*. Both heaven and hell know that Satan is merely a figurehead, a puppet, an exile. It is only mankind who seems unaware that the "roaring lion" (1 Peter 5:8) has had his teeth pulled and is on a leash to the "Lion of the tribe of Juda" (Revelation 5:5). The only power left to him is the power of persuasion, but this was all that he needed in the Garden of Eden to con man into departing from God's control to Satan's control. Oh, that God could cause today's Church to examine the display case containing all these trophies of Christ's victory over Satan!

Jesus "hath delivered us from the power of darkness . . ." (Colossians 1:13). Satan's only power or authority in our lives is what we choose to give him by believing his persuasive lies and submitting to his pretended authority. He may still wear the uniform of a general, but all rank has been stripped from him. He may still parade an army of sorts, but their weapons have been taken from them. He may talk like a mighty contender, but he is only a "roaring lion," not an attacking one.

Through the action of *luō*, *katargeō*, and *apekduomai*, Jesus has delivered us from all of Satan's control, and He has translated us into His Kingdom of light. Jesus has delivered us from—into. He is a complete Deliverer, and has become our King.

8

Jesus, Our King

". . . and hath translated us into the kingdom of his dear Son" (Colossians 1:13).

In Paul's day, monarchies were the rule; in our day they are the exception to the rule. Paul understood the authority of a king and the ramifications of a kingdom. Accordingly, he declares that we have not only been delivered out of the power of darkness but "translated . . . into the kingdom of his dear Son." Paul consistently taught that God did not send Jesus Christ merely to save us from sin, but He sent Him to bring us into the Kingdom of heaven. Spoiling Satan so we could be delivered from his power was only step one in God's program for His people. God never lost sight of His original goal to form a "kingdom of priests" (Exodus 19:6), even though Israel rejected the concept and settled for the tribe of Levi as their substitutes, and eventually rejected their unseen God as their king, demanding that one of their own be enthroned as monarch over them. But God's purposes are never changed by man's choices. ". . . Thy will be done in earth, as it is in heaven," Jesus taught us to pray (Matthew 6:10).

Although God gave men the desires of their hearts in Saul and subsequent earthly kings, He also gave the prophets insight into the coming divine King—the promised Messiah (literally "the Anointed King"). Balaam saw His star and scepter (Numbers 24:15–17), Isaiah saw Him born of a virgin with the title "Prince of Peace" (Isaiah 9:6,7), while Zechariah exhorted Israel, "Rejoice greatly, O daughter of Zion; shout, O daughter of Jerusalem: be-

hold, thy King cometh unto thee . . ." (Zechariah 9:9). The Psalmist wrote much of this coming King, declaring, "Yet have I set my
king upon my holy hill of Zion" (Psalms 2:6), and devoting complete psalms as special foreshadowings of the messianic King
(Psalms 24, 45, 72, 89, and 110). Israel was so steeped in this messianic hope that when the angel Gabriel announced to youthful
Mary that she had been chosen as the vessel through which this
divine King would be born, there was no resistance, arguing, or
even questioning. She seemed to understand the message without
great explanations. The King was expected.

Jesus Came as King

When the Magi arrived in Jerusalem after their star-led pilgrimage, their question was, "Where is he that is born King of the
Jews?" (Matthew 2:2). From the moment of His birth, the scholars
called Him "King." Herod's rage caused him to seek to destroy this
contender for his throne by killing all of Bethlehem's children two
years old and younger. If he had not believed the wise men he
would not have felt so threatened by this proclamation, but he did
believe them.

Jesus was considered a King by James and John as they inter-
ceded with Him, through their mother, for positions of authority
and power in His Kingdom (Matthew 20:21). Nathanael hailed
Jesus as "King of Israel" the first time he met Him (John 1:49),
while Peter proclaimed, "Thou art the Christ [Messiah], the Son of
the living God" (Matthew 16:16). There seemed to be no doubt in
the minds of the disciples that Jesus was a King.

Subsequent to this, Jesus was almost compelled by the multitude to set up an immediate earthly kingdom following the miraculous feeding of the multitude. "When Jesus therefore perceived
that they would come and take Him by force, to make him a king,
he departed again into a mountain himself alone" (John 6:15).
Later the worshipers among this multitude loudly proclaimed
Him as their King during the triumphal march on Palm Sunday,
as they waved palm fronds and loudly chanted, "Blessed is he that
cometh in the name of the Lord: Blessed be the kingdom of our fa-

ther David, that cometh in the name of the Lord: Hosanna in the highest" (Mark 11:9,10). The people saw Him as King and were more than willing to submit to His rulership.

At His arrest, Jesus was charged by the chief priests with claiming to be a King, for when they brought Him to Pilate they said, "We found this fellow perverting the nation . . . saying that he himself is Christ a King" (Luke 23:2). Taking Jesus into the judgment hall, Pilate asked Jesus, "Art thou the King of the Jews?" and Jesus answered, "Thou sayest it" (Luke 23:3). No matter what the many false witnesses testified, the charge was that Christ claimed to be a divinely appointed King.

Furthermore, Pilate convicted Jesus as a King. Although he tried to get out of it, political pressure and expediency made it imperative for Pilate to consent to the wishes of the religious rulers. At the whipping post, "the soldiers platted a crown of thorns, and put it on his head, and they put on him a purple robe, And said, Hail, King of the Jews!" (John 19:2,3). Following this, Pilate sat in the judgment seat at Gabbatha and said unto the Jews, "Behold your King! . . . Shall I crucify your King?" (John 19:14,15). Jesus was convicted as charged!

At Calvary Jesus was crucified as a King. The title of conviction that was placed over the cross at the orders of Pilate read, "JESUS OF NAZARETH THE KING OF THE JEWS" (John 19:19). To be certain that the reason for Christ's crucifixion was understood by all who witnessed it, Pilate had this inscription written in Hebrew, Greek, and Latin, the three major languages of that day, the languages of religion, culture, and government.

God's purpose in Christ's coming was that He be King. People recognized this, but rejected Him (John 1:11). He was called King by the Magi, considered King by the disciples, almost compelled to function as King by the multitudes, crowned King by the Palm Sunday worshipers, charged as a King by the chief priests, convicted as King by Pilate, and crucified as King by the Roman soldiers. But once again man's actions could not change God's attitudes. God raised Jesus from the dead and named Him "KING OF KINGS, AND LORD OF LORDS" (Revelation 19:16), and "set him at his own right hand in the heavenly places, Far above all principality, and power, and might, and dominion, and every name that is named, not only in this world, but also in that which is to come: And hath put all things under his feet, and gave him to be the head over all things to the church" (Ephesians 1:20–22). Jesus is King by God's actions, not by man's acceptance of those actions.

The world has seen enough kings who have been dethroned, dispossessed, deported, and deprived of the kingdom, and high society has its share of pretender kings, but Jesus Christ is a King not only in name; He is a King in fact! He has not been dethroned; He has been enthroned. He is not merely a King in our minds; He's God's King over God's Kingdom.

Jesus Preached the Kingdom

Mr. I. H. Marshall observes in the *Zondervan Pictorial Encyclopedia:*

The word "kingdom" is found fifty-five times in Matthew, twenty times in Mark, forty-six times in Luke and five times in John. When allowance is made for the use of the word to refer to secular kingdoms and for parallel verses of the same sayings of Jesus, the phrase "the kingdom of God" and equivalent expressions (e.g. "kingdom of heaven," "His kingdom") occur about eighty times. The word "king" is used also of Jesus with considerable frequency but only rarely with reference to God.

Jesus wasted no time in proclaiming His Kingdom and His Kingship. ". . . Jesus came into Galilee, preaching the gospel of the kingdom of God, And saying, The time is fulfilled, and the kingdom of God is at hand: repent ye, and believe the gospel" (Mark 1:14,15). Similar reports are given in Matthew 4:23 and 9:35. Christ's basic message was quite concise and contained four fundamental points. Point one: The King is here; "The time is fulfilled." Point two: It is now; "The Kingdom of God is at hand." Point three: "Repent"; and point four: "Believe the gospel."

This simple message established Christ as King, earth as part of His Kingdom, repentance as a necessity for entering that Kingdom, and released faith ("believe") as a prerequisite to receiving the benefits of that Kingdom. Thousands of sermons have been preached on this subject, and hundreds of books have been written on it, but because Christ thoroughly understood it, He could say it in one simple sentence.

Perhaps the uniqueness of Christ's message is that He did not magnify His position as King; instead, He underscored the fact that His Kingdom was a Gospel—"good news." The true Gospel, or the full Gospel, as some like to call it, is not that Christ died for our sins in order to deliver us from Satan's kingdom; it is that subsequent to that release we have been invited to enjoy the protection and provisions of the Kingdom of heaven. This is what Paul is talking about when he writes, "Who hath delivered us from the power of darkness, and hath translated us into the kingdom of his dear Son" (Colossians 1:13). We are brought from one control to another; from one provision to another; from one kingdom to another; and *this* is the Gospel. The force of the verb that defines this action is "good news," for it is obvious that it has been done by another on our behalf. Translators speak of it thus: "translated us into . . ." (KJV), ". . . has removed us into . . ." (TCNT), "re-established us in . . ." (PHILLIPS), and "transplanted us into the kingdom of His beloved Son" (CONYBEARE).

It is this Gospel, this good news, this Gospel of the Kingdom that was the message of Jesus, and He did not modify it even at the very end, for when Pilate asked Him, ". . . Art thou the King of the Jews? Jesus answered, My kingdom is not of this world: if my kingdom were of this world, then would my servants fight, that I should not be delivered to the Jews: but now is my kingdom not from hence. Pilate therefore said unto him, Art thou a king then? Jesus answered, Thou sayest that *I am a king. To this end was I born,* and for this cause came I into the world, that I should bear witness unto the truth . . ." (John 18:33,36,37, italics added).

The Nature of That Kingdom

Perhaps the most alarming part of Christ's preaching was that He declared that the Kingdom was "now" and "here." The Jews in

His day were totally dominated by the cruel occupational government of Rome, so the harsh realities of life prohibited their comprehension of a present Kingdom of God. They had a strong hope
for the future and faithfully awaited the coming of their Messiah,
David's Son, who would establish a material kingdom on the lines
of the Davidic or Solomonic kingdom with all the pomp, ceremony, and courtly rituals associated with earthly kings. To them,
it defied credulity to accept the teaching that the Kingdom was at
hand; they were subjects of Rome with status just one step above
vassal slaves.

Men's hearts are the same at all times and everywhere, for we
are as ready to become "prisoners of hope" (Zechariah 9:12) as
they were. All Christians expect Christ to be crowned King, but
the Bible declares, "The kingdoms of this world *are* become the
kingdoms of our Lord, and of his Christ; and he shall reign for ever
and ever," and, "For the kingdom is the Lord's: and he *is* the governor among the nations" (Revelation 11:15; Psalms 22:28, italics
added). The Bible does not look forward to the reign of Jesus; it
declares it to be operational right now. Today's generation may
not seem to know it, and the governments of the world may choose
to ignore it, but Jesus "must reign, till he hath put all enemies
under his feet" (1 Corinthians 15:25). One day all godless ideolo-
gies will learn that Jesus Christ is King of Kings, to whom they
must surrender and submit or be broken and destroyed.

This nearly universal ignorance of Christ's Kingdom operating
in the present affairs of men may lie in man's blindness to a spiritual realm. Even believers in Christ sometimes find it difficult to
accept that there is another world or realm coexistent with this
world to which, by God's help, we can tune in from time to time. It
seems easier to place God many light-years above us in space than
to accept the reality of a spiritual Kingdom coexistent with our
material kingdom. But it is so. Scientists have shown how easily
this could function by demonstrating that in the arrangement of
the building blocks of the universe, the atoms, there is more space
between the atoms than the space the atoms occupy. That is to say,
there is more empty space between the atoms in a table than there

is solid material. If we could control the alignment of these atoms, it should be possible to pass a chair through a table, or a person through a wall, without any conflict whatever. Jesus demonstrated this after His Resurrection, when He walked through a locked door to meet with His mourning disciples in the upper room.

Without really understanding this, we accept its reality. Why, then, should it be so difficult for us to believe that the angels of God are with us, and that God's Holy Spirit abides with the inhabitants of Christ's Kingdom even when they're not aware of Him?

In speaking of the Resurrection, Paul says that while it is a natural body that is put into the earth, it is a supernatural body that comes out of the grave; the terrestrial becomes celestial. He also points out that there are two different levels of glory: "The glory of the celestial is one, and the glory of the terrestrial is another" (1 Corinthians 15:40). We earthbound creatures cannot seem to break through the barriers into the spiritual realm without the help of one on the other side, but those glorified beings of God's celestial order have no difficulty reaching into our dimension.

We are so consistently tuned to Channel Earth that we rarely bother to switch to Channel Heaven. But that heavenly Kingdom is as near to us as the natural kingdom, just as multiple channels of TV and radio broadcasting fill the room simultaneously. When properly attuned, "Ye are come unto (1) Mount Sion; (2) unto the city of the living God, the heavenly Jerusalem; (3) and to an innumerable company of angels; (4) to the general assembly; (5) to the church of the firstborn, which are written in heaven; (6) and to God the Judge of all; (7) and to the spirits of just men made perfect; (8) and to Jesus the mediator of the new covenant; (9) and to the blood of sprinkling, that speaketh better things than that of Abel" (*see* Hebrews 12:22–24).

The Kingdom of God is separated into two distinct divisions: not Catholic and Protestant, but human and spiritual . . . here and there . . . earth and heaven . . . saints present and saints departed. This is not an antagonistic division but a division necessitated by contrasting realms. But this division is more artificial than real, for the Kingdom is the same; it is merely the subjects who are different, and their difference is more a matter of levels of spiritual maturity than difference of character.

Through the entire New Testament, spirituality is listed as the prevailing characteristic of Christ's Kingdom: "The kingdom of God is not meat and drink; but righteousness, and peace, and joy in the Holy Ghost," Paul said (Romans 14:17). While earthly kingdoms are usually based on material power, the basal factor of Christ's Kingdom is righteousness. Similarly, while the ruling principle in earthly kingdoms is selfish or national aggrandizement, in the Kingdom of Christ it is *truth*. Since righteousness and truth occupy such a prominent place in Christ's Kingdom, it is to be expected that this Kingdom would be distinguished by its spirituality, and it is. The inhabitants of this Kingdom are spiritual men and women; its laws are spiritual laws; its work is spiritual work; all the forces emanating from it, operating through it, or centering in it, are spiritual.

This glorious Kingdom is demonstrated and declared a Kingdom of grace (Matthew 20:1–16), of power (1 Corinthians 4:20), of glory (1 Thessalonians 2:12), and is called "heavenly" (2 Timothy 4:18). It has an unworldly character to it; it has a universality; it touches heaven and earth; it is eternal. Facets of its nature and its desirability are illustrated in many of Christ's parables, but Jesus emphasized its availability to men right now. We do not await our death and resurrection to enter this Kingdom; we are born into it by action of the Spirit of God. We are not waiting for His Kingdom—we are surrounded by it, engulfed in it, and dominated by it. We share in its benefits right now, while we wait for this righteous Kingdom to take dominion and authority over all other kingdoms and reign supreme—to come with visible display.

The Dominion of King Jesus

Jesus Christ is no figurehead—He is *Monarch* in the full sense of true monarchy. He is "King of all the earth" (Psalms 47:7), and "he is the governor among the nations" (Psalms 22:28). He is spoken of as the Head of the body which forms His Church, exercising complete and absolute control. He is also revealed as the Shepherd of the sheep, with powers of life and death, and He is declared seated at the right hand of God, ruling and reigning in authority and power.

Christ rules with unlimited authority. He is not subject to a parliament, congress, or any governing body. He testified, "All power is given unto me in heaven and in earth" (Matthew 28:18), and Peter said of Him, "Who is gone into heaven, and is on the right hand of God; angels and authorities and powers being made subject unto him" (1 Peter 3:22). Paul declared:

> Wherefore God also hath highly exalted him, and given him a name which is above every name: That at the name of Jesus every knee should bow, of things in heaven, and things in earth, and things under the earth; And that every tongue should confess that Jesus Christ is Lord, to the glory of God the Father.
>
> Philippians 2:9–11

There is no realm of authority that has been denied Christ Jesus.

Similarly, Christ rules with unlimited dominion. During His time on earth He demonstrated His dominion *over men*. They couldn't trip, tempt, or trick Him. "Never man spake like this man" (John 7:46), was their testimony. Jesus turned their hatred into love and caused businessmen to forsake their former way of life to follow Him. Multitudes flocked to isolated places to listen to Him. Equally, Jesus demonstrated His dominion *over the elements*. He calmed the storm, multiplied bread and fish to feed the hungry, walked on water, filled nets with fish, until the disciples asked, "What manner of man is this, that even the winds and the sea obey him!" (Matthew 8:27). Repeatedly, Jesus demonstrated His dominion *over sickness* in healing all manner of sickness, opening blinded eyes, unstopping deafened ears, and even raising the dead. He did this with a touch, with a word, with a prayer, and sometimes with a sigh. He healed them singly and en masse, so great was His dominion. Furthermore, He demonstrated His dominion *over Satan* during His entire ministry. He resisted temptation, cast out demons, destroyed Satan's works, and at His Ascension He stripped Satan of all authority and power. What a King! What dominion! Every area of life is under His control.

Entering That Kingdom

When Jesus began His public ministry by preaching about the Kingdom of heaven, He listed two prerequisites for entrance: repent and believe. While acknowledging the Kingship of Christ also implies the acceptance of the kind of behavior which He prescribes—submission to the concrete demands of the King (Matthew 5:19), and the production of a character more righteous than that of the scribes and Pharisees (Matthew 5:20)—these ethics of the Kingdom are not a condition of entry to the Kingdom, for God does not lay down certain qualities of character as entrance requirements. Jesus' Gospel was a message of grace, and the response of men to that proffered grace is to repent and believe (Mark 1:15).

Entering into the Kingdom of God requires a decision on man's part. *Repent* is translated from a Greek military term which means "about face"—a 180-degree change in direction. Repentance, then, is not an emotional reaction; it is an obedient response, so we cannot repent with our mouth but only with our life. While godly sorrow may move man's emotions, which in turn motivate his mouth to confession, repentance requires a complete change of direction. This turn from our way to His way also requires faith, for His way is a great unknown to us. ". . . He that cometh to God must believe that he is, and that he is a rewarder of them that diligently seek him" (Hebrews 11:6). Man need not change the character of his life to enter Christ's Kingdom—only its direction. Repentance mixed with faith are the resident visas in our passport.

It is the will of God for us to enter into the Kingdom of heaven; that's why He sent His Son, Jesus, to declare to men that the Kingdom is NOW . . . it's HERE . . . it's SPIRITUAL . . . it's COEXISTENT . . . and it's OBTAINABLE.

The principles of this Kingdom, its bylaws, its ethics, its teachings, its present and future benefits, its behavior code, and its standards, are the subject of much of the New Testament. Yet one of the most striking things about the preaching of the Early Church is the way in which the message of the Kingdom of God fell into the background, and its place as the theme of preaching was taken by the person of Jesus Himself. Even for Paul, the King became more important than the Kingdom.

Christ is King of truth, King of salvation, King of grace, King of peace, King of righteousness, King of glory, King eternal, King of saints, King of the ages, King of Kings, and ". . . on his head [are] many crowns . . ." (Revelation 19:12). Small wonder, then, that Paul coupled our deliverance "from the power of darkness" and our translation "into the kingdom of his dear Son" with, "In whom we have redemption . . . even the forgiveness of sins" (Colossians 1:13,14).

9

Jesus, Our Redeemer

"In whom we have redemption . . ." (Colossians 1:14).

In speaking of Paul's writings, Peter says, ". . . in which are some things hard to be understood . . ." (2 Peter 3:16). If he had had access to the Book of Revelation, I am certain he would have included John in that statement, for although the book is declared "The Revelation of Jesus Christ" (Revelation 1:1), some of the pictures of Jesus contained in the book are difficult for us to grasp. Notable among them is the picture of Jesus as the Lamb "that was slain" (Revelation 5:6,12). Nearly thirty times He is called the Lamb, yet He is seen seated on the throne with authority, power, majesty, dominion, and great honor. Every response to Him is the response given to a king, and His position and performances are clearly kingly. Is this a conundrum, or is it merely a dual representation of the offices of Christ? Paul also has coupled this binary nature of Jesus here in Colossians chapter one, for, as we have seen, he projects Jesus as being a King with a Kingdom, and with only a colon for separation, he speaks of Christ as being our Redeemer through the shedding of His blood. Why does the Scripture correlate king and dying lamb?

Postulations of Redemption

In our society, we recognize the obligations of power. Before we appoint a man to a position in government, we run a check on him and have a hearing, at which time the man's background and behavior are carefully studied. Some conduct that is accepted of a private citizen is unacceptable in a public officer, for with the conferring of power comes a transferring of obligation, and the greater the power, the greater the obligation.

This is a genuinely Christian concept rooted in Scripture, and it is generally ignored in non-Christian countries. Since it is God Himself who has taught us that the greater the power the greater the obligation, we must assume that God recognizes that He is the most obligated Being in the universe. If God holds man under heavy obligations to correctly use the power of controlling the forces already at work in the world, how much greater are the obligations on the Creator who brought these forces into being!

Furthermore, men are not in the world by their own choice; it was God who called human beings into existence and endowed them with reproductive powers that function more on blind impulse than in moral responsibility. From the Fall of Adam until the most recently born baby, all persons have been conceived and born with sinful natures and have developed in sinful surroundings. Even before they learn to walk and talk, they are captive slaves of sin, and no matter what their station in life may become, none will ever be able to redeem himself from that slavery. If there is to be redemption it must come from God, and the Bible seems to indicate that God accepts the obligation to redeem those whom He has sent into the world. This would imply not a forced redemption, but an offered redemption. Man is free to accept or reject God's offer, but the divine provision of Redemption is fundamentally a discharge of the obligations on the part of God Himself.

The picture of Jesus as the sovereign Lord and the slain Lamb is consistent with this concept of divine obligation. As the King of Kings He has absolute power, and therefore He has absolute obligation. His discharge of that obligation was to descend from divinity to humanity and die as our paschal Lamb. He is both King and Redeemer for all who will accept His Redemption.

One need not be a Greek scholar to understand the meaning of the word *redeem*, for the verb in both Greek and English conveys the solid concept of a purchase. It is to buy back or pay a ransom. We use it of kidnaped victims being rescued by the paying of a demanded ransom, and we refer to the stores that accept bonus stamps given by retail merchants as "redemption centers."

The idea of redemption in the Old Testament starts with the management of property, for the law made provision for the buying back, or redemption, of property that was sold or lost through indebtedness (Leviticus 25:26). From this concept, Redemption was enlarged to embrace the general sense of deliverance throughout the Old Testament. God is seen as the Redeemer of Israel in the sense that He was the Deliverer of Israel (Deuteronomy 9:26). This Redemption or deliverance encompassed all forms of evil or national misfortune (Isaiah 52:9), plagues (Psalms 78:35), or calamities of any sort (Genesis 48:16). This was based on the general thought that God had both a claim upon Israel (Deuteronomy 15:15) and an obligation toward Israel (1 Chronicles 17:21). Israel belonged to Him, and it was His prerogative to intervene in the life of Israel to redeem her. Even beyond this, the prophets seemed to sense that it was God's obligation to redeem covenant Israel (Hosea 3).

In the New Testament the idea of Redemption has more of a suggestion of ransom. Men are seen as held under the curse of the law (Galatians 3:13) and of sin itself (Romans 7:23), and totally unable to release themselves from the bondage. The redeemer must purchase their deliverance on their behalf. While the progression of revelation does not negate the idea of God's delivering man from misfortune and distress, the scriptural emphasis moves more and more to the concept of deliverance from sin, for all of the New Testament writers project sin as the chief disturber of man's welfare.

In essence, then, the premise that is developed in the Scriptures is that *redemption* is deliverance from the power of an alien dominion and the subsequent enjoyment of the resulting freedom. The *redeemer* is the one who possesses the right or who exercises the right of redemption.

Pictures of Redemption

Long before the New Testament doctrine of Redemption was developed, God amply illustrated it in His dealings with Israel and

in the laws which governed Israel's dealings with herself. After the
people of Israel walked through the Red Sea, Moses sang, "Thou
in thy mercy hast led forth the people *which thou hast redeemed:* thou
hast guided them in thy strength unto thy holy habitation" (Exodus 15:13, italics added), calling attention not only to the Redemption but to the Redeemer. God had a prior claim upon Israel,
and His act of Redemption delivered her people from the alien
dominion of Egypt and reestablished their relationship to Him
who was their rightful Lord.

In effecting this Redemption, God had repeatedly plagued
Egypt, culminating in the death of the firstborn in the land. Ex-
emption from this death penalty was granted to those families who
entered into a blood covenant with God by placing the blood of a
slain lamb on the lintel and doorposts of their home. Although
unslain, these firstborn males, both man and beast, were now considered the property of Jehovah and must now live lives totally devoted to God's service or be redeemed through the payment of a
prescribed price (Exodus 13:2,11–16).

Later, as Israel entered into the covenant of the law, God made
provision for a kinsman who had the right of avenging or redeeming the blood of a victim (Numbers 5:8; 1 Kings 16:11). Furthermore, this kinsman (*gouail*) could redeem property that a near rela-
tive had lost, for in Israel the land belonged to God and the
families possessed the right only to use the fruit of the land. If a
family sold the land, or if the father died without leaving an heir,
the land was returned to the family at the year of jubilee (Leviticus
25:8–17), or the nearest kinsman had the right and responsibility
to redeem the property, that is, to satisfy the debt and return the
ownership to the rightful heir. The story of Boaz and Ruth is a
classic illustration of this; for in it we see the redemption not only
of land but also the redemption of a family lineage, for God had
also provided that the near kinsman of someone who had died
without leaving a male heir was obliged to marry the widow of the
deceased in order to preserve the family name and property rights.
Boaz entered into this levirate marriage with Ruth, and their son
was called a redeemer by grandmother Naomi because his birth
delivered her from the reproach she had incurred because her fam-

ily had no surviving male heir (Ruth 4:14). Boaz, the redeemer, ransomed their land, their heritage, and their reputation because he was near of kin, was financially able, and was morally willing. What a picture of Jesus, our Redeemer.

The Psalmist gives us a picture of the limits inherently imposed upon a *gouail* in saying, "None of them can by any means redeem his brother, nor give to God a ransom for him: (For the redemption of their soul is precious, and it ceaseth for ever:) That he should still live for ever, and not see corruption" (Psalms 49:7–9), and Jesus asks: "For what is a man profited, if he shall gain the whole world, and lose his own soul? or what shall a man give in exchange [as a ransom] for his soul?" (Matthew 16:26).

Of course, ju: ˙ as the architect's scale model can never fully portray the grandeur and beauty that will characterize the completed structure, so the many pictures of Redemption that illustrate Christ's work and its results only suggest the fullness that was yet to come. But they were a foretaste, a preview, and a pledge of better things to come. Being possessors of the greater enables us to visualize even more in those miniatures than those who were active participants in them. "Better is the end of a thing than the beginning thereof . . ." (Ecclesiastes 7:8).

The Principles of Redemption

We've already seen that Redemption involves persons in bondage, a prior claim, a provided person, a prescribed price, and a persuadable payee. Obviously, man is in slavery to sin; God has a prior claim by right of creation; Christ is designated our *gouail;* vicarious death is the price; but who is the persuadable payee? To whom is this payment made?

The majority of the Early Church fathers (Irenaeus, Origen, Gregory of Nyssa, Ambrose, Augustine, and so on) viewed Redemption as a judicial transaction in which Jesus gave up His life to the devil in payment for mankind's release. Gregory Nazianzen, opposing this concept, treated Redemption as a conflict between Christ and Satan for the possession of man rather than as a judicial transaction. Later, Athanasius developed the theology of Redemption to the concept that the divine *Logos* assumed human nature and gave Himself up to death because the justice and veracity of God demanded the death of mankind, as He had threatened, for sin. This was further refined by subsequent theologians and adopted by the Reformers.

If we view Redemption quite objectively, we can easily make of it a commercial transaction between Christ and God, which affects us only insofar as we are the object of it. This, of course, raises the question of the necessity and possibility of any such transaction.

Neither here in Colossians nor in any of his other writings does Paul attempt to answer the question of to whom the ransom was paid. He seems to see the process as something which took place toward us and in our favor, not as something which took place toward God and His favor, for Paul always sees God as integrally involved in the cross and not apart from it. Accordingly, then, Paul does not view God as the one who receives but as the one who acts in the cross of Jesus.

While it is true that the earliest usage of the words for Redemption associates them with the payment of a price, a ransom, and this is equally true of the biblical teaching of Redemption, the Scriptures are virtually silent about the one to whom ransom is paid. The focus of attention is consistently on the sufficiency of the payment made by Christ, not the one to whom the payment was made.

The *International Standard Bible Encyclopedia* makes this point crystal clear in saying:

> If we look for the common thought in all the Christian statements of God's part in redemption we find it in this: that in all these statements God is conceived of as doing all that He can do for the redemption of man. If in earlier times men conceived of the human race as under the dominion of Satan, and of Satan as robbed of his due by the deliverance of man and therefore entitled to some compensation, they also conceived of God Himself as paying the ransom to Satan. If they thought of God as a feudal lord whose dignity had been offended by sin, they thought of God as Himself paying the cost due to offended dignity. If their idea was that a substitute for sinners must be furnished, the idea included the thought of God

Himself providing a substitute. If they conceived of the universe as a vast system of moral laws—broken by sin—whose dignity must be upheld, they thought of God Himself as providing the means for maintaining the dignity of the laws. If they conceived of men as saved by a vast moral influence set at work, they thought of this influence as proceeding, not from man, but from God. The common thought in theories of redemption then, so far as concerns God's part, is that God Himself takes the initiative and does all He can in the discharge of the obligation upon Himself. Each phrasing of the doctrine of redemption is the attempt of an age of Christian thinking to say in its own way that God has done all that He can do for men.

". . . thou has redeemed me, O Lord God of truth" (Psalms 31:5) seemed to satisfy David, and it has been the ringing testimony of the Church throughout the present dispensation. When time has been consummated and we stand in the presence of God in the eternities, our paean of praise will be, "Thou . . . hast redeemed us to God by thy blood out of every kindred, and tongue, and people, and nation; And hast made us unto our God kings and priests: and we shall reign on the earth" (Revelation 5:9,10).

The Purpose of Redemption

In my book *Let Us Enjoy Forgiveness,* I say:

We must realize that the whole background to the word *ransom,* both in Greek and in English, is "captivity." It is always concerned with retrieving, emancipating, freeing, or liberating a person or a possession from some hostile power that has taken possession of him or it.

We were born to the slavery of sin; we bankrupted our inheritance and became servants of the satanic system. Ours was a living death, for both in Adam and in action we traded access to the Tree of Life for a sample of the Tree of Knowledge of Good and Evil. But God had a plan! Quoting again from *Let Us Enjoy Forgiveness:*

We who were born to slavery, we who had never known the joys of being free from sin, have been ransomed, redeemed, delivered from our bondage both by Christ's paying the price and by God's destruction of Satan's power. We have been freed from the captivity of the past and any subsequent fear of future captivity. We've been emancipated and avenged, all through the operation of God's forgiveness.

God's plan for us was forcibly demonstrated in His redeeming Israel *out of* Egypt *into* the Promised Land. God liberates us out of bondage and leads us into freedom, for His release involves a renewal of all that had been lost to us. "As in Adam all die, even so in Christ shall all be made alive," Paul declares (1 Corinthians 15:22).

The glorious plan of God's was at least threefold. First, He purposed to redeem us from the curse of the law (Galatians 3:13) and establish us in grace. This releases us not only from the death penalty of the law but also from the legal prescriptions of the Old Testament dispensation (Galatians 4:1–5), and from the requirement of obedience to the law as a way of life (Galatians 2:16,19). Now we "walk in the Spirit," are "led of the Spirit," and "live in the Spirit" (Galatians 5:16,18,25).

The second purpose in God's plan of Redemption was to redeem us from the guilt and power of sin. Paul told Titus, ". . . our Saviour Jesus Christ . . . gave himself for us, that he might redeem us from all iniquity, and purify unto himself a peculiar people, zealous of good works" (Titus 2:13,14). Sin is an insidious, sinister power that controls men through their passions and destroys them through their sense of guilt. Christ redeems us not merely from the ultimate penalty of sin but from its presence, power, pollution, and guilt. "Sin shall not have dominion over you," we are assured (Romans 6:14). Even if there were no heaven, and, thank God there is, being released from the captivity of sin would be heavenly. How excitedly we used to sing the little gospel chorus, "Oh, this is like Heaven to me!"

But there is still a third purpose in God's Redemption of men, and while it is absolutely dependent upon the first two, it is actually the outgrowth or maturing of them. God sent men a Redeemer in order that they might live life to its fullest extent. Peter tells his readers that they were "redeemed . . . from your vain conversation [literally, conduct, manner of life] received by tradition [that is, from the routine of custom]" (1 Peter 1:18). The word *vain* means "empty and unsatisfying." Life before Redemption in Christ is futile and vain; it is groping or fumbling after something it can never find; and with all its strivings it does not come into contact with reality. But through Christ's Redemption we come into contact with reality, we receive a new source of life, and we walk "in newness of life" (Romans 6:4).

The ultimate aim of Redemption is to bring men to the fullest use and enjoyment of life both now and in eternity. This is tacitly implied in the very word *redeem,* for the prisoner redeemed by money payment comes out of prison to the light of day; the slave comes out of slavery into freedom, and the one who is ransomed is restored to his home and friends. They are both delivered from a curse and thereby released unto a larger and fuller life. This enjoyment of life is the prime purpose of the redemption. Jesus, our Redeemer, declared, "I am come that they might have life, and that they might have it more abundantly" (John 10:10). He brought us out of sin and ransomed us from the law in order to bring us into abundant life. His life replacing our life becomes abundant life.

The Person of Redemption

Redemption is a work of divine mercy accomplished by the Incarnation, obedience, death, and Resurrection of Christ, which involves the total Godhead and envelops the entire life of the redeemed. No work of God is more complete than His work of Redemption, for it has judicial, ethical, physical, intellectual, moral, and social aspects to it, and Jesus is the Provision for each of them.

The *judicial side* of Redemption satisfies the law of God. The law says, "The soul that sinneth, it shall die" (Ezekiel 18:4,20), and Jesus became that dying soul, for Paul wrote, "Christ hath redeemed us from the curse of the law, being made a curse for us . . ." (Galatians 3:13). Whatever claims God's law had against us have been totally satisfied in the work of Jesus at Calvary's cross.

But Redemption is far more than an act that satisfies God, for in its *ethical side* Christ has redeemed us from all unrighteousness, as His own possession, purifying us unto good works (Titus 2:14); He has overcome the world whose temptation leads us into evil, and has also completely broken the power of the prince of this world— the devil. Not only is God's law satisfied; our lives are purified. God is seen as just while we are justified.

As to the *physical aspect* of our Redemption, Jesus has released our total persons—spirits, souls, and bodies—from the power of sin. By the same substitutionary work at Calvary that bought our souls and spirits back from darkness, our bodies are brought out of sickness: "with his stripes we are healed" (1 Peter 2:24; Isaiah 53:5)—and when Christ returns He will raise the dead, insuring them against further pain or death and imparting eternal life in a glorified body similar to the one Jesus received when He rose from the dead.

Besides these aspects, the perfect Redemption that Jesus brings to men acts upon the *intellectual nature* of that man, delivering him from darkness unto light, and Jesus, Himself, is that Light. It is sin that has clouded the minds of men, and when Jesus removes man from that sin, man's intellect is released from bondage and enabled to develop without the hindrances of the satanic kingdom. Redemption does not restrict man's reasoning faculty; it releases it. Freed of sin, sickness, and satanic influence, man's mind soars beyond the limits of his little world into the unexplored area of God's heavenly Kingdom.

Nevertheless, a released mind without corresponding liberation of man's moral nature would be at best only partial, and at worst it could be devastating. Jesus has redeemed our *moral nature* in delivering our will from the bondage of sin and enduing it with the power to choose and execute works of righteousness. Christ redeems us from the world, the flesh, and the devil; faith in Him overcomes the world (1 John 5:4).

Furthermore, Redemption affects the *social life* of the redeemed. The object of Redemption, socially, is to set men in relation to each other as members of a family. The Psalmist David discerned this, for he wrote, "God setteth the solitary in families: he bringeth out those which are bound with chains: but the rebellious dwell in a dry land" (Psalms 68:6). We need to remember that God began with a family, Abraham, which He subsequently enlarged into a nation, but sin and selfishness consistently rebel against the rules of society in that every person wants to do his or her own thing. The work of Redemption breaks down every form of selfishness and makes us willing to be dependent upon others and dependable to them. The change from sinner to saint also involves change from individual to integration; the released slave becomes one of many sons. The loneliness of captivity is replaced by the loveliness of family relationship, so that Christ's redeeming love will have an object to which to express love—a family—for unexpressed love will die, and introspective self-love will destroy. We need this family relationship for a healthy outlet of the love we have received, and through Jesus we are born into this family of God.

This perfectly complete Redemption is costless to mankind. We are not bailed out by a bondsman to whom we are indebted for both the bond and interest; we are freely forgiven. The price is paid on our behalf by another, but we are never billed for it. Redemption is God's own affair (John 3:16), and the cross was the price it cost Jesus. There are no works of righteousness, acts of penance, deeds of greatness, or gifts of gold expected of or accepted from man as a condition to Redemption. Paul summarizes it by saying, "Therefore as by the offence of one judgment came upon all men to condemnation; even so by the righteousness of one the free gift came upon all men unto justification of life" (Romans 5:18).

This is not to imply, of course, that the transition from status under the law to sonship with Jesus is accomplished by a mere declaration of God, for it was not by the declaration of God but by the death of Jesus that we were ransomed—not merely released. God did not act as Pilate in releasing a Barabbas; He acted as Boaz in buying back what had been lost and relating to us as a husband in order to bring forth fruit of righteousness. No human mind can calculate what this cost Jesus. We cannot conceive what it was like to take the omnipresent Christ of God and incarcerate Him in a human body, nor can we imagine what it was like for one who had been eternally sinless to have all the sins of the world laid upon

Him at Calvary. Our Redemption cost an incalculable price, but Jesus paid it all.

Nevertheless, although this Redemption is costless to man, it does not automatically pertain to all men, even though the literal concept of a ransom is seen as paying a price for a man's deliverance, whether the man wants it or not. It is natural to assume that any man in prison or in slavery would be overjoyed at being redeemed, but in dealing with men whose lives are formed in sin and completely used to sin we cannot safely make this assumption. As any witness for Christ has quickly learned, the dreadfulness of sin is basically in the sinner's love of sinning. Anyone who hates sin finds it difficult to realize that other persons love sin, revel in sin, and live for the pleasures of sin. They not only do not want to be rescued from sin; they will fight anyone who attempts such a rescue.

Nowhere does Scripture teach that men are redeemed by fiat. God's purchased Redemption is merely provisional until man exercises his will to participate in it. God unlocks the prison door, but we must walk out into freedom. If we choose to die in our sins God will not violate that choice, but He will consistently seek to motivate us to change our wills. This is where Christ is gloriously our Redeemer, not only as having paid the purchase price but also in being the prime motivational force to change our will. The Scripture does not say that God commendeth His program of Redemption to us; it says, "God commendeth His *love* toward us, in that, while we were yet sinners, Christ died for us" (Romans 5:8). God does not bring us into Redemption by displaying His fiat, but by stirring our feelings. It is not legal briefs but divine love that stirs the will of the sinner. God first attracts us unto Himself, and then releases us from ourselves, and His method of attraction is Jesus (John 3:16). Therefore, Jesus came both to settle an account and to sell the program, for He is the purchaser and promoter of Redemption. He delivered us and then demonstrated the gloriousness of that deliverance, seeking to attract us into accepting His free gift. First He entices us into His love, and then He extradites us out of our bondage into His limitless freedom. Jesus is certainly the complete Redeemer.

Even the measure of the completeness of our Redemption is to be found in the absolute perfectness of our Redeemer, Jesus Christ. A little later in his letter to the Colossians, Paul writes, "For in him [Jesus] dwelleth all the fulness of the Godhead bodily. And ye are complete in him . . ." (Colossians 2:9,10). Not only does Redemption release us to pursue a full life but it also relates us intimately to Christ very much as a grafted branch is related to the tree. Freed from sin and fused to Christ, we become beneficiaries of all the fullness of God that dwells in Jesus. Little wonder, then, that Hebrews speaks of "so great salvation; which at the first began to be spoken by the Lord, and was confirmed unto us . . . God also bearing . . . witness, both with signs and wonders, and with divers miracles, and gifts of the Holy Ghost, according to his own will" (Hebrews 2:3,4).

And this complete Redemption is also a continuous Redemption, whose ultimate end is to make men like Jesus—to infuse into men the life that is in Christ Jesus, our Redeemer. This will take all of time and much, if not all, of eternity. But it can and will be done because "the image of the invisible God" (Colossians 1:15) "is able to do exceeding abundantly above all that we ask or think, according to the power that worketh in us" (Ephesians 3:20). We have been, we are being, and we shall ever be redeemed because Jesus Christ bought our Redemption for us, brought that Redemption to us, and became that Redemption unto us. Jesus is our Redeemer who lives, ministers, and loves as a manifestation of the image of God.

10
Jesus, the Image of God

"Who is the image of the invisible God . . ." (Colossians 1:15).

Paul, whose initial confrontation with Jesus was audible rather than visual, declares here that God's Christ is the image (in Greek *eikon*), the exact likeness or representation of the invisible God. To Timothy, Paul called God "the King eternal, immortal, invisible . . ." (1 Timothy 1:17). Paul's conception of the divine realm was that it is as real and specific as our natural world, for he refers to thrones, dominions, principalities, and powers (Colossians 1:16), and always maintains an awareness of angels, glorified beings, and a literal city (Hebrews 12:22–24). He doesn't visualize God's Kingdom as ethereal or nebulous; he sees it as literal and tangible. He merely concedes that it remains invisible to mortal eyes because "the god of this world hath blinded the minds of them which believe not . . ." (2 Corinthians 4:4). Our inability to see does not negate the reality of the divine realm, but it does greatly limit our ability to comprehend or appreciate it.

The Need for an Image

Too often we're like the four blind men who tried to visualize an elephant through their sense of touch. The one holding the tail declared that an elephant was like a small inverted bush, and the one touching a leg insisted that the elephant was like a tall tree trunk! The blind man running his hands across the mammoth sides of the elephant described it as a large stucco wall, while the sightless explorer who had a hold on the trunk insisted vehemently that it should be obvious to everyone that an elephant was like a writhing snake. Similarly, our concept of God is fragmented, distorted, and severely limited because of our inability to see the invisible God, for since the days of the dispersal at the Tower of Babel men have been unable to see into God's heaven.

That God has sought to reveal Himself is obvious, for all creation tells us that there is a supreme Being—a Creator. David wrote, "The heavens declare the glory of God; and the firmament sheweth his handywork. Day unto day uttereth speech, and night unto night sheweth knowledge" (Psalms 19:1,2). Every culture of mankind throughout the history of the world has marveled at the canopy of stars on a dark, clear night, but have any of them come to a knowledge of God through such observations? We loosely speak of worshiping the God of nature as a euphemism for enjoying the beauty of our world, but all of God's glorious handiwork does not reveal God's nature and character; at best it testifies of an intelligent Being, very much as an expensive wristwatch testifies of the existence of a watchmaker.

Paul declares:

> . . . what may be known about God is plain to them, because God has made it plain to them. For since the creation of the world God's invisible qualities—His eternal power and divine nature—have been clearly seen, being understood from what has been made, so that men are without excuse.
>
> Romans 1:19,20 NIV

God's handiwork could have revealed God, but men contented themselves with the creation without seeking the Creator. They were so overawed at the macrocosm that they failed to see its testimony of the Maker.

Man—the Image of God

In God's unfolding program of self-revelation, He chose to recreate Himself in miniature, visible form. "God said, Let us make man in our image, after our likeness. . . . So God created man in his

own image, in the image of God created he him . . ." (Genesis
1:26,27). God created a triune man comprised of a spirit, soul, and
body that enabled him to have a God-consciousness, a self-con-
sciousness, and a world-consciousness. This "child" possessed the
"likeness" of God and was formed in the very "image" of the most
high God. It was expected that as he discovered himself he would
also discover God; that is, that the knowledge of the scale model
would give insight into the One after whom he was modeled.

Initially this seems to have worked, for in the cool of the evening
Adam walked and talked with God in the beautiful Garden of
Eden. The wisdom of God so abounded in Adam that he named
all of the birds of the air, the beasts of the field, and the fish in the
sea, and God entrusted him with authority over all of creation and
endowed him with such purity of heart and mind as to make him
absolutely shameless. Adam was so like God that he fellowshipped
with Him with no sense of distance or hesitancy. They were alike
in nature, but different in quality. It was Father and son enjoying
one another, for regardless of how great the distance between their
levels of development and maturity may have been, they were akin
in their essential nature.

However, man defiled this divine image through disobedience to
God's commands. Experimenting with the forbidden fruit of the
Tree of the Knowledge of Good and Evil, Adam introduced sin
into the human race. Immediately his spirit was so separated from
its union with God that God had to call in the garden, "Adam,
where art thou?" (*see* Genesis 3:9). Already Adam's soul was so
filled with shame and fear that he had covered himself with leaves
and hidden himself from God (Genesis 3:10). Furthermore, his
body immediately became subject to the processes of death; the
dominion and authority of man was revoked, and he was driven
from his Edenic meeting place with God.

"Ye shall be as gods," Satan had said (Genesis 3:5), but what a
price to pay for seeking a shortcut to being godlike. Adam already
had the nature; it needed only maturation. Unwilling to mature
into the full image of God, Adam sought to achieve instant god-
likeness by substituting knowledge for relationship, but instead of
increasing his likeness to God, he deformed, defiled, and degen-

erated the small image of God in which he had been created. Unfortunately sin has not finished its work in the human race, for man has become more warped and contorted from God's likeness day after day. No longer can any of us look within ourselves to see what God is like; we must look to God to see what we should be like, but to our sin-blinded eyes God is invisible. Even saintly Moses was not allowed to see God, for God answered his request by saying, "Thou canst not see my face: for there shall no man see me, and live" (Exodus 33:20). Sin has both blinded our eyes to God and has so deformed our nature that we cannot stand to look upon God; it would be death dealing to us.

Literary Revelation of God's Image

As bad as it is that sin cost man this divine image, it inevitably produced serious confusion about God in men's minds because of this marred earthly image. Mythology reveals how deformed this image of God had become, for men pictured God to be like their baser selves, only with sufficient power and impunity to do anything He desired. God was seen as proud, haughty, lustful, cruel, unjust, impure, and sensual. Accordingly, He was to be feared, entreated, and regularly propitiated, even if it entailed human sacrifice.

Of course all of this violated God's expression of self-revelation both in creation and in mankind, but sin had so warped men's minds that they couldn't see the true for their preoccupation with the false, so God tried to reveal Himself vocally through the prophets and instrumentally through the pages of the written Word of God. He illustratively describes Himself as "a consuming fire" (Deuteronomy 4:24; Hebrews 12:29), "love" (1 John 4:8), "light" (1 John 1:5), and "holy" (1 Peter 1:16). None of these, however, gives an adequate picture of the living God, for a "consuming fire" conjures up visions of uncontrollable destruction, "love" is confused with carnal lust; "light" is viewed as cosmic energy, and "holiness" seems to be a forbidding "otherwiseness" to which we cannot easily relate.

Through the written Word, God revealed His basic attributes of omniscience, omnipresence, omnipotence, and eternity, and by repeated acts of love and mercy He demonstrated His filial love for mankind. We read at length of His provision, protection, guidance, and goodness toward His covenant people, and learn that He is faithful and just in all of His ways. God also sought to introduce Himself to men in the use of many compound names for Himself, such as *Jehovah-jireh* ("The Lord will provide" [Genesis 22:14]), each of which reveals a different facet of God's nature.

Yet in spite of all that the thirty-nine books of the Old Testament declared, described, and demonstrated about God, He remained the invisible God, unapproachable and incomprehensible to most persons, for they could not translate the stories and statements about God into corporeal concepts about Him. Jehovah continued to be such an awesome mystery that the Jews would not even pronounce His name; they substituted a euphemism. To them God was sacred but shapeless, real but remote.

Jesus, the Image of God

Because of man's inability to rise high enough to adequately comprehend God, Jehovah determined to lower Himself to man's level in order to reveal Himself in human flesh. Accordingly, "When the fulness of the time was come, God sent forth his Son, made of a woman, made under the law" (Galatians 4:4). The angel Gabriel had told this woman, Mary, "Thou . . . shalt call his name JESUS. He shall be great, and shall be called the Son of the Highest . . ." (Luke 1:31,32), establishing from the very beginning that this miraculous conception would gestate into a supernatural God-man, Jesus Christ. He came not merely as saviour and substitute; He came primarily as a revelation and demonstration of God to mankind—the very "brightness of his glory, and the express image of his person . . ." (Hebrews 1:3).

The Last Adam—the Second Man

Because Adam and his sin-deformed progeny failed so completely in comprehending and revealing the invisible God, the divine councils of heaven decreed an end to the lineage of Adam.

"And so it is written, The first man Adam was made a living soul; the *last* Adam was made a quickening spirit" (1 Corinthians 15:45, italics added). Jesus came as the last of the Adams, in order to eradicate once and for all the irreversible failure of man to reveal the divine Father, for although millions of people had been born between Adam and Jesus, God's image in them was so marred by sin that it was defaced, defiled, and deformed unrecognizably.

When God chose to reveal His image in the *second* man, He gave him a different nature—a higher nature. The first man was made in the image of God as Lincoln's image is struck on our penny, but the second Man is the image of God as Lincoln's son bore his father's image. "Christ is the image of God," Paul affirms (*see* 2 Corinthians 4:4). Whereas Adam was a man made in the image of God, Jesus was God, "bearing the human likeness, revealed in human shape . . ." (Philippians 2:8 NEB). Instead of trying to elevate man into the divine image, God reversed the process by beginning with the image of God and placing it in human flesh. Thus Adam was replaced by Jesus, who not only ended the Adams but also began an entirely new lineage by becoming the "second man" (1 Corinthians 15:47)—the God-man.

Although Mary, the Magi, Simeon, and Anna were able to see the divine side in the infant Jesus, it was actually during the brief period of His ministry that the Father was best revealed in His Son. Philip, a disciple of Jesus, asked:

> Lord, shew us the Father, and it sufficeth us. Jesus saith unto him, Have I been so long time with you, and yet hast thou not known me, Philip? he that hath seen me hath seen the Father. . . .
>
> John 14:8,9

In what way had they seen the Father in Jesus?

Everywhere Jesus went He spoke words of pardon, peace, release, deliverance, healing, and comfort. Dr. Luke tells us, "All bare him witness, and wondered at the gracious words which proceeded out of his mouth . . ." (Luke 4:22). Even His enemies declared, "Never man spake like this man" (John 7:46), yet Jesus affirmed, "He whom God hath sent speaketh the words of God . . ." (John 3:34).

The works of Jesus were mighty works evidencing authority in the realms of nature, the demonic, the total human being, and the divine; still Jesus declared, "The Son can do nothing of himself, but what he seeth the Father do: for what things soever he doeth, these also doeth the Son likewise" (John 5:19). Furthermore, Jesus told the Jews that all judgment that He exercised had been committed to Him by the Father (John 5:22). The works of Jesus were so revealing of the Father that "Jesus cried and said, He that believeth on me, believeth not on me, but on him that sent me. And he that seeth me seeth him that sent me" (John 12:44,45).

At the end of His earthly ministry, in His high-priestly prayer in the upper room, Jesus assured the Father, "I have glorified thee on the earth: I have finished the work which thou gavest me to do . . . I have manifested thy name unto the men which thou gavest me out of the world . . ." (John 17:4,6), and later in Gethsemane He reaffirmed His responsibility to conform completely to the image of God by praying, ". . . not my will, but thine, be done" (Luke 22:42).

No sin ever marred the image of God in this second Man until the sins of the entire world were laid on Jesus at Calvary, and even there He demonstrated God's image in freely forgiving the soldiers who crucified Him and in assuring the repentant thief that he would meet Jesus in Paradise.

In Christ's generation and geographic area men saw the image of God, for it walked among them, talked to them, demonstrated divine compassion upon them, and stirred some of them to a hope of glory that had been absent from the nation for many generations. Even the Roman centurion in charge of the crucifixion saw God in Jesus, for he declared, "Truly this was the Son of God" (Matthew 27:54).

Where the first man ignominiously failed, the second Man gloriously succeeded!

But this revelation of God's image didn't end with the impalement of Jesus on a cruel Roman cross, for God triumphantly resurrected Him from the dead and:

... raised him high and gave him the name which is above all other names so that all beings in the heavens, on earth and in the underworld, should bend the knee at the name of Jesus and that every tongue should acclaim Jesus Christ as Lord, to the glory of God the Father.

Philippians 2:9–11 JERUSALEM

This acclamation of Jesus Christ as Lord became the theme of the Early Church's message. Peter boldly proclaimed it on the day of Pentecost in the concluding statement of his sermon when he said, "Therefore let all the house of Israel know assuredly, that God hath made that same Jesus, whom ye have crucified, both Lord and Christ" (Acts 2:36), and Paul, Peter, James, John, and Jude consistently used this title for Jesus in their New Testament books.

Perhaps today's generation sings *He Is Lord* with a mental concept of Jesus being in authority over their lives, or ruler of the Church, but the Jews in Peter and Paul's time had a far higher image than this. In their day it was unthinkable to pronounce the sacred name of God. When copying the Scriptures, the scribes would totally bathe themselves before writing that sacred name, and then would cut a new quill with which to transcribe that unspeakable name. But although they would write it, they would not read it aloud. Instead, they substituted the word *Lord*. When the apostles applied the title *Lord* to Jesus they were declaring that He was very God of very God—the One who was viewed as so sacred that none dared speak His name. Little wonder that such preaching stirred deep resentment and anger. The Jews had crucified Jesus as an imposter king, and now His followers were declaring that He was not only a king but the Messiah (Christ) and a physical, visible manifestation of the Eternal Living One called Jehovah (Yahweh). He was declared the Lord to whom they gave sacrifice and worship. To the Jews this was blasphemous, and they diligently sought to kill all who proclaimed such sacrilegious slander. Among the most blatant of these persecutors was Saul of Tarsus, who was stopped by a divine light on the road to Damascus and challenged by "a voice saying unto him, Saul, Saul, why persecutest thou me? And he said, Who art thou, Lord? And the Lord said, I am Jesus whom thou persecutest . . ." (Acts 9:4,5). One glimpse of the glory coupled with the melodious message of the voice so convinced Paul that this Jesus was indeed the Lord, the Christ, God made manifest to man in the flesh, that he used this title for Jesus nearly 270 times in his writings.

Redeemed Men Bear God's Image

Paul told the Church at Thessalonica that he prayed consistently for them "That the name of our Lord Jesus Christ may be glorified in you, and ye in him, according to the grace of our God and the Lord Jesus Christ" (2 Thessalonians 1:12). He well knew that this Jesus, the Revealer of the Father, also became the Redeemer of mankind, and in that redemption is restored back into the image of God. Jesus, the second Man, colonized an entire race of people who would continue to reveal the image of the invisible God. These citizens are seen in plural relationship to each other, but they are united with Christ. Sometimes they are called Christ's "body," "bride," or "family," and other times they are referred to as "a royal priesthood," "a holy nation," and "a peculiar people." But whatever their structural association or spiritual title, their purpose is to "shew forth the praises [Greek: *artē*—"manliness" or "virtues"] of him who hath called [them] out of darkness into his marvellous light" (1 Peter 2:9).

Accordingly, Paul dares to write, "A man . . . is the image and glory of God . . ." (1 Corinthians 11:7); "And as we have borne the image of the earthly, we shall also bear the image of the heavenly" (1 Corinthians 15:49), and affirms that when we behold the glory of Jesus in the heavenlies, "We . . . are changed into the same image from glory to glory, even as by the Spirit of the Lord" (2 Corinthians 3:18).

Perhaps the Church manifests the image of God as the moon reflects the light of the sun, but it is an earthly demonstration of a divine likeness—God is seen in the transformed lives of former sons of Adam. It is a return to the miniature, the scale model, but now it is not warped by sin. God's character is seen in the Church when the fruit of the Spirit ripens, and His authority and power are revealed when the gifts of the Spirit operate.

Some have said that the Church is the image of God as a photograph is an image of a person. Even if we are that limited, at least we are a visible evidence that the pictured One does exist, for that is what a photograph testifies.

Nonetheless, even when the Church is radiant and healthy she is a most incomplete revelation of the invisible King. To complete that revelation, God has arranged for Jesus Christ to return to earth once again as a complete manifestation of the divine image. When Paul said that Jesus was the image of God (Colossians 1:15), he was declaring that Jesus is an essential manifestation and embodiment of the Father, for in "image" there is the idea of derivation from an original. It is not mere likeness that is predicated, but God is represented (however imperfectly) as the original and Christ as the copy. Thus, the invisible God becomes visible to man. At the Second Coming of Jesus Christ, "Every eye shall see him" and "every knee shall bow before" the "Christ, who is the image of God" (*see* Revelation 1:7; Philippians 2:10; 2 Corinthians 4:4).

At the first revelation of Jesus, as seen in the Gospels, He bore the image of the Father in His ways, works, words, and will, but at the second revelation of God's Christ, as shown in the Book of Revelation, mankind will see that ". . . in Christ all the fullness of the Deity lives in bodily form" (Colossians 2:9 NIV). All of God's nature, attributes, will, and works combined with God's holiness, wisdom, dominion, and authority will be seen in Jesus, who will continue to be the visible, physical demonstration of the invisible God throughout all eternity, for the Book of Revelation shows that it is Jesus seated upon the throne; Jesus acting in judgment upon the earth; Jesus responding to the prayers of the saints; and Jesus welcoming the redeemed into eternal glory.

Jesus, as the image of God, has perfect equality with the Father in respect to substance, nature, and eternity, and He came and will return to reveal this to mankind. He, the Creator, became the creature in order to bring the creation into harmonious fellowship with God. This He has done, is doing, and will continue to do throughout all of eternity.

11

Jesus, the Creator

"Who is ... the firstborn of every creature: For by Him were all things created. ... And he is before all things, and by him all things consist" (Colossians 1:15–17).

The revelation of the deity of Jesus Christ is not accommodated by a man's intellect until it has been apprehended by his spirit. Like Peter, we get hung up intellectually on the humanity of Jesus, however great it was. Peter had eaten, slept, walked, and talked with this Jesus and had even shared in some of His miraculous works, but it took a divine revelation before he could declare, "Thou art the Christ, the Son of the living God. And Jesus answered and said unto him, Blessed art thou, Simon Bar-jona: for flesh and blood hath not revealed it unto thee, but my Father which is in heaven" (Matthew 16:16,17). The pivotal point of the Bible revelation of God is not only that God was in Christ but also that Jesus Christ is God, for if Jesus Christ is not God, then the only God we have is a vague representation of our own mind. Happily, Paul continues to add point after point in his irrefutable argument for the divinity of Jesus Christ, yearning to awaken in the saints at Colossae the "spirit of wisdom and revelation in the knowledge of him" (Ephesians 1:17).

Oswald Chambers reminds us in his book *Still Higher for His Highest:*

Just as Jesus Christ is the final revelation of God, so the Bible is the final revelation interpreting Him. Our Lord Jesus Christ (The Word of God) and the Bible (the accompanying revelation) stand or fall together; they can never be separated without fatal results.

What is the Bible record about this Lord Jesus Christ? In his letter to the Church at Philippi Paul summarized it so succinctly in saying:

> His state was divine, yet he did not cling to his equality with God but emptied himself to assume the condition of a slave, and became as men are; and being as all men are, he was humbler yet, even to accepting death, death on a cross. But God raised him high and gave him the name which is above all other names so that all beings in the heavens, on earth and in the underworld, should bend the knee at the name of Jesus and that every tongue should acclaim Jesus Christ as Lord, to the glory of God the Father.
>
> Philippians 2:5–11 JERUSALEM

Theologians refer to this passage as the *kenosis* or the self-emptying of Christ. Christ stripped Himself of His divine attributes in becoming Jesus, but after His obedient death on Calvary's cross, God restored all that had been set aside. By the Ascension God raised Christ Jesus to glory so that He was again seen as omnipotent, omniscient, omnipresent and eternal. All the supernatural power, so restricted in His earthly life, becomes omnipotence; all the wisdom and insight, so precious but so limited during His life on earth, becomes omniscience; all the limited presence of Jesus, confined to a small geographical area during the days of His flesh, becomes omnipresence, so that He is with His people everywhere and at all times, and the extreme pressure that condensed God to a span in time was released so that Christ Jesus was again an active agent in eternity. The Ascension and exaltation of Jesus Christ returned Him to His full position in the Godhead.

Jesus Was Prior to Creation—"The Firstborn"

Paul deliberately couples Jesus' being "the image of the invisible God" with being "the firstborn of every creature" (Colossians 1:15). Other translators handle the Greek word *prototokos*, which the King James translators translated as "firstborn," variously: "First-born and Head of all creation" (TCNT); "His firstborn Son who existed before any created thing" (WILLIAMS); ". . . his is the

primacy over all created things" (NEB); "He was born before creation began . . ." (PHILLIPS); and ". . . He existed before God made
anything at all" (LB), are some of them. The variations stem from
the fact that the word has a., its Greek root the word *protos,* which
basically means "foremost" (in time, place, order, or importance);
hence it is translatable as "superior," "beginning," "best," "chief,"
"first (of all)," or "former."

Before His Incarnation Jesus was the image of the invisible God
as the Word (John 1:1–3); during His Incarnation Jesus was God's
image as the God-man on earth; and after His Ascension He continued to be the image of the invisible God by returning to His position as "the firstborn of every creature" (verse 15). This phraseol-
ogy is Jewish, for the Jews termed Jehovah as the firstborn of all
the world, or of all the creation, to signify His having created or
produced all things. It was a common phrase in Paul's day, de-
noting God's preexistence and pointing God out as the cause of all
things. Obviously Paul uses that phrase in the same way concerning Jesus and amply illustrates it in the phrases that follow: "For
by him were all things created . . . all things were created by him,
and for him: And he is before all things, and by him all things
consist" (Colossians 1:16,17). Even the Psalmist seemed to grasp
this truth when he sang, "Also I will make him my firstborn,
higher than the kings of the earth" (Psalms 89:27).

It is the clear teaching of the Bible that heaven and earth have
not existed from all eternity; they had a beginning in God's act of
Creation. But this expression, "firstborn," or "firstbegotten,"
places the beginning of Jesus Christ long before the world began.
We read in *Clarke's Commentary* that one Christian philosopher of
many years ago argued:

> As all *creation* necessarily exists in *time,* and had a *commencement,* and
> there was an *infinite duration* in which it *did not* exist, whatever was
> *before* or *prior* to that must be *no part of creation;* and the Being who
> existed prior to creation, and *before all things*—all existence of every
> kind, must be the unoriginated and eternal God: but St. Paul says,
> *Jesus Christ was before all things;* ergo, the apostle conceived Jesus
> Christ to be truly and essentially God.

In his introductory statements, the writer to the Hebrews said:

The son is the radiance of God's glory and the exact representation
of his being, sustaining all things by his powerful word. . . . So he
became as much superior to the angels as the name he has inherited is superior to theirs. For to which of the angels did God ever
say, "You are my Son; today I have become your Father"? Or
again, "I will be his Father, and he will be my Son"? And again,
when God brings his firstborn into the world, he says, "Let all
God's angels worship him". . . . But about the Son he says, "Your
throne, O God, will last for ever and ever, and righteousness will be
the scepter of your kingdom. . . ."

Hebrews 1:3–6,8 NIV

There can be no question that the inspired author was convinced
of the eternity of Jesus Christ, and that He had priority with su-
perlative dignity to everything in the universe. As stated in the Ni-
cene creed, ". . . Begotten of his Father before all worlds."

In declaring Jesus "the first-born into the world" (RSV), the reference cannot be to the Incarnation but to the divine preexistence
of Christ. While we have no reason for thinking that the human
soul of Christ existed before the Incarnation, it is plainly taught
here by Paul that the divine nature of Christ existed long before
Creation was conceived. During His days on earth, Jesus said the
same of Himself in declaring, "Verily, verily, I say unto you, Before Abraham was, I am" (John 8:58). This would mean, among
other things, that all those divine characteristics which are so
beautifully revealed in Jesus of Nazareth were not produced for
the first time in the New Testament days—they existed in the age
of Moses and even at the Creation of the world. It follows, then,
that the whole scheme of nature and the government of the world
must be in accordance with what we know of Christ. He was before
all, He produced all, and He is in all. This would also mean that
there is no ground in this passage on which to build the theory of
the creatureship of Christ. He was not created; He was the Creator!

In the New Testament, the term *firstborn* is applied five times to
Christ (Colossians 1:15,18; Romans 8:29; *see* Hebrews 1:6; Revela-

tion 1:5). While speaking primarily of Christ's eternity and superiority over all of creation, it may also be seen figuratively reminding us of the place which the firstborn occupied in a Hebrew family, for by virtue of the order of his birth, the firstborn had priority and a certain supremacy over the other family members and received a double portion of the inheritance. Our Lord Jesus Christ has ample priority existing "before Abraham," before all creation, and "before all things" (Colossians 1:17). Because of His absolute preexistence, He has supremacy over all things; therefore He enjoys more than the firstborn's double portion. He has all the rights, responsibilities, and benefits of the firstborn, and the Father jealously guards this position of His Son.

Jesus Is the Power of Creation—". . . by Him . . ."

From the very first chapter of the Bible we are taught that God is the Author of all existence: "In the beginning God created the heaven and the earth" (Genesis 1:1). It pictures a personal God calling into existence by His almighty will, manifested by His Word, and executed by His Spirit, things which had no being. It presents a Creator distinct from His Creation, speaking into existence a universe, not eternal, but which had a beginning in time, and doing it in successive periods—the six days—and in progressive order—beginning with the lowest element, matter, and continuing by the plant and animal life, terminating by man made in God's image.

The Hebrew word for God here in Genesis 1:1 is *Elohim.* The Hebrew word *El* means "the strong one, the almighty"; *Elohim* is the plural for "God" as *cherubim* is the plural for "cherub" and *seraphim* is the plural for "seraph." *Elohim* is the first hint of the trinity in the Godhead. It is not God the Father in the act of Creation, but God the Father, God the Son, and God the Holy Spirit bringing forth something out of absolutely nothing. This is amply illustrated in the first verses of Genesis, chapter one. After being told that the original Creation had undergone some sort of a cataclysmic upheaval that left it "without form, and void; and darkness was upon the face of the deep" (verse 2), we are told, "And the

Spirit of God moved upon the face of the waters. And God said, Let there be light: and there was light" (verses 2,3). Here is the Father willing, the Spirit moving, and the Word producing. The prime power in Creation was the Word of God: ". . . God said. . . ."

In the prologue to his Gospel, John writes, "In the beginning was the Word, and the Word was with God, and the Word was God. The same was in the beginning with God. All things were made by him; and without him was not any thing made that was made" (John 1:1–4). The rest of this chapter establishes conclusively that this Word (*Logos*) was indeed Jesus. While it is true that Creation can be ascribed to God the Father, as it is in Romans 11:36, it is equally true that God never acts immediately; He always acts through the agency of the Son. John and Paul are very explicit on this subject: "All things were made by him [the Word]; and without him was not any thing made that was made" (John 1:3); and "[Through] whom [His Son] also he made the worlds" (Hebrews 1:2), they declare.

"For by him were all things created . . ." (Colossians 1:16), Paul wrote. Most other translators change it to "In Him," which is more consistent with Paul's usage of this Greek preposition. But whether "by" or "in," Paul declares that Jesus Christ is the Creator of all things. He does not state that Christ Jesus created officially or by delegation, for as Creation requires absolute and unlimited power or omnipotence, there can be but one Creator; for it would be impossible to have two or more Omnipotents, Infinites, or Eternals. To suggest that Christ Jesus was merely delegated to create the universe would imply a Being conferring the office and delegating such power, and that Being to whom it was delegated would be a dependent Being, therefore not unoriginated and eternal. But no limited being could produce a work that necessarily requires omnipotence. Furthermore, if omnipotence was delegated, quite obviously he to whom it was delegated must not have had it before, and he who delegates it ceases to have it and consequently would cease to be God, while the other to whom it was delegated would become God, because such attributes as those with which he is supposed to be vested are essential to the nature of God.

How careful we must be in expressing our concepts of the Trinity. "The Lord our God is one Lord," God declared (Deuteronomy 6:4). Christ Jesus is not an inferior God, or second in command to God; He is the exact expression of Almighty God, who is "the image of the invisible God . . ." (Colossians 1:15). This is expressed quite clearly in the Book of Hebrews:

> Long ago God spoke in many different ways to our fathers through the prophets [in visions, dreams, and even face to face], telling them little by little about his plans. But now in these days he has spoken to us through his Son to whom he has given everything, and through whom he made the world and everything there is. God's Son shines out with God's glory, and all that God's Son is and does marks him as God. He regulates the universe by the mighty power of his command. . . .
>
> Hebrews 1:1–3 LB

So it is neither God nor Jesus acting independently one from the other in the act of Creation, but it is God in Christ, for God created with His Word, and Christ Jesus is God's *Logos,* Word, and the divine Word carries in Him the archetypes of all existences, so that in Him all things in heaven and earth were created. By virtue of His relation to God, Christ is the *ground* of Creation, both in heaven and on earth, and at the same time He is its *means* and its *end.* Christ Jesus is, therefore, supreme over the universe.

To underscore this, Paul lists four pairs of divisions in the universe: "Heaven and earth; visible and invisible; thrones, or dominions, or principalities, or powers: all things were created by him, and for him" (*see* Colossians 1:16). He created all spheres, whether in the heavens above or the earth beneath. There is no locality that He did not bring into existence. Beyond that He created the nature of all things; some visible, and some invisible. Furthermore, He created all the inhabitants in these spheres, whether thrones, lordships, principalities, or dominions. Paul affirms that the invisible beings of the worlds above us, however lofty their names or mighty their powers, are His creatures as much as the lowliest objects within our sight.

Because the invisible world is such an unknown to us, Paul uses two pairs of descriptions where the first is greater than the second—thrones or dominions; principalities or powers. Both express an office exercised toward the creatures; but thrones and dominions seem rather to be so called because of their relation to God, so far as they display His majesty (Ephesians 1:21). It is quite impossible for us to know fully what these terms convey in connection with the various hierarchies of heaven, for the Scriptures have not given us much understanding of that glorious realm, but they do seem to point to gradations of being and to distinctions of official glory. Still, all these invisible beings, so illustrious as to be seated on *thrones,* so great as to be called *dominions,* so exalted as to be considered *principalities,* so potent as to merit the designation of *powers,* were created by the Son of God; and they all acknowledge His supremacy and glory. The highest position in creation is infinitely below Him, and there is neither majesty nor renown that equals His. ". . . all things were created by him, and for him" (Colossians 1:16).

Jesus Is the Purpose of Creation

Not only is Jesus prior to all Creation and the power of the Creation; He is also the purpose of that Creation. He was preexistent to Creation and the producer of it, but He also has preeminence in all of Creation. As Lightfoot put it, "He is the Source of its life, the Centre of all its developments, the Mainspring of all its motions."

In his commentary on Colossians, Adam Clarke writes:

Creation is the proper work of an infinite, unlimited, and unoriginated Being; possessed of all perfections in their highest degrees; capable of knowing, willing, and working infinitely, unlimitedly, and without control: and as creation signifies the production of *being* where all was *absolute nonentity,* so it necessarily implies that the Creator acted *of* and *from* Himself; for as, previously to this creation, there was no being, consequently He could not be actuated by any *motive, reason,* or *impulse, without Himself;* which would argue there was some being to produce the *motive* or *impulse, or to give the reason.*

Apart from Christ, there would have been no Creation at all. He was the reason for it. He was the First Cause and the Final Cause, the Alpha and the Omega of Creation. The term "in Him" includes the following truths "by Him" and "for Him," "through Him and unto Him." Everything in Creation and in history was planned for the glory of our blessed Lord Jesus Christ. This world, with its forests, mountains, lakes, and flowing meadow streams, with all of its flowers, fruits, birds, and butterflies, was made so beautiful because it was Christ's world. Other worlds, peopled by the heavenly hosts, were also created, that His glory might be revealed to and through them. ". . . all things were created . . . for him" (Colossians 1:16), Paul affirms. It is an unscriptural philosophy that teaches that all things were made for man, for even man himself was created unto Christ's glory (Ephesians 1:12). Christ Jesus, not man, is the great end of Creation. As surely as all Creation emanated from Him, so does it all converge again toward Him. The eternal Word is the goal of the universe, as He was the starting point. ". . . thou hast created all things, and for thy pleasure they are and were created" (Revelation 4:11).

There can be no doubt that *heaven* was created for Him, for it is the place of His special residence and the future home of the redeemed. Quite obviously the *angels* were created for Him, for they are messengers of His mercy, executors of His will, and executioners of His vengeance. Equally, *hell* was created for Him, for it is the prison of His justice. The *earth* was created for Him, for it was the scene of His Incarnation and atoning death, and is the seat of His mediatorial kingdom. Furthermore, the human race was created for Him, for man was created in His image, and is recreated into that image. As J. B. Phillips translates it, "Through the Son God made the whole universe, and to the Son he has ordained that all creation shall ultimately belong" (Hebrews 1:2 PHILLIPS). To the Church in Corinth, Paul quoted the Psalmist in writing: "For the earth is the Lord's and the fulness thereof" (1 Corinthians 10:26), but David added, ". . . the world, and they that dwell therein" (Psalms 24:1).

God's firstborn is the natural Ruler, the acknowledged Head of God's household. He is Heir of all things. He is Creation's supreme and absolute Lord. He brought all creatures out of nothing, and by His own will established the degree of being each should possess; and it is fitting that He should have unlimited sovereignty over all. In the three prepositional phrases Paul uses here in Colossians, chapter one, the circle of Creation is traced. "In Him" (*see* verse 16) carries us back to the beginning of Creation. "By Him" (*see* verse 16) leads us along its process; "for Him" (verse 16) points us to its end.

Jesus Is the Perpetuator of Creation

". . . by Him all things consist" (*see* verse 17), Paul asserts. Phillips translates this seventeenth verse, "He is both the first principle and the upholding principle of the whole scheme of creation." God's Son of His love is the Conserver as well as the Creator of all things. Apart from Him, atomic fission would explode the universe into fragments. But for Jesus, all things would fall asunder and go back into nothingness. All the laws of the universe which regulate and give stability to things subsist in Christ and are nonexistent out of Him. His continued existence is really the guarantee for the sun's rising every morning. It will rise so long as He, who made it, has an end in its rising, for all things have consistence and persistence only in His existence and in His ends. There is no other basis on which things can proceed toward the final consummation.

We are comfortable in knowing that every effect depends upon its cause, and cannot exist without it; therefore, Creation, which is an effect of the power and skill of the Creator, can only exist and be preserved by a continuance of that energy that first gave it being. Hence, Christ Jesus, as the Preserver, is as necessary as Christ the Creator was to the original production.

It has been suggested that the apostle speaks here the language of philosophy, for in Plato and Aristotle the term *consist* (consistence) is found expressing the essentially philosophical conception of the inherent unity, in virtue of which the universe is such and forms a single, correlated whole. Paul declared that this unifying principle was the *Logos,* the image of God, to whom alone fullness belongs. Christ Jesus is the cement and the bond of things and He

has chained and woven together everything so that it is itself absolutely full of Christ Jesus. "In him we live, and move, and have our
being . . ." Paul told the Athenians on Mars Hill (Acts 17:28).

". . . by him all things consist" (verse 17) clearly declares that all
of creation holds together and coheres by the action of Jesus
Christ. He is the principle of cohesion in the universe. He impresses
upon Creation that unity and solidarity which makes it a cosmos
instead of a chaos. As Lightfoot suggests, the action of gravitation,
which keeps fixed things in their places and regulates the motion of
moving things, is an expression of Christ's mind.

The universe found its completion in Jesus, and is sustained and
preserved every moment by the continuous exercise of His almighty power. All things hang on Christ; if He withdrew His upholding hand, everything would run into confusion and ruin. He is
the center of life, force, motion, and rest; around Him all things
revolve. He imposes their limits, gives to them their law, strikes the
keynote of their harmonies, and blends and controls their diverse
operation, for He is the all-perfect in the midst of imperfection,
and the unchanged in the midst of change.

Jesus Christ, the beloved Son of God, is the cornerstone of the
universe as well as of the Church. Behind the laws of nature we see
the mind of Christ, and above the Church of the living God we see
the mind of Christ. He who is head of all creation is also head of
the Church, and just as the pulses of universal life are regulated
and controlled by the throbbings of the mighty heart of Jesus
Christ, so the universal Church is regulated and controlled by the
living involvement of Jesus Christ, its head and its heart.

12

Jesus, the Head
of the Church

"And he is the head of the body, the church: who is the beginning, the firstborn from the dead; that in all things he might have the preeminence" (Colossians 1:18).

After unfolding how Christ holds the position of absolute priority and sovereignty over the whole universe, Paul proceeds to point out Christ's relation to the Church, as its supreme Head and primal, life-giving Source.

In His high-priestly prayer, Jesus told the Father, "I pray for them: I pray not for the world, but for them which thou hast given me; for they are thine" (John 17:9). Although "the earth is the Lord's, and the fulness thereof; the world, and they that dwell therein" (Psalms 24:1), following His mediatorial work at Calvary the New Testament focuses upon the concern of Jesus Christ for that select, chosen group of people who have accepted Christ's death as their own and have chosen to become His "peculiar people" (Titus 2:14). This collective group is pictured variously, sometimes seen as Christ's bride emphasizing their love relationship to their Bridegroom. Other times they are seen as the body of Christ on this earth emphasizing their service or ministry response to Jesus, and other times they are seen as the Church, a "holy habitation," or a "temple." But however they may be designated, they are one and the same group of "called out" believers who have submitted to Jesus Christ as the Authority over their lives.

Jesus Is the Head of the Body

Before speaking of the Church, Paul chooses to establish Christ Jesus' headship over the body of believers and declares that "He is the head of the body. . . ." In writing of the Resurrection, Ascension, and exaltation of Jesus Christ in his letter to the Ephesians, Paul says "And hath put all things under his feet, and gave him to be the head over all things to the church, Which is his body, the fulness of him that filleth all in all" (Ephesians 1:22,23), thereby reversing the order of Colossians, but until there is an animated body there cannot be an actuated Church.

Over the years, much controversy has prevailed as to what constitutes the Church, and it seems that the more worldly the Church became the more confused the definition and the more bitter the controversy became. Still, the New Testament idea of the Church is not difficult to understand, for it is the whole body of the faithful in Christ Jesus, who are redeemed and regenerated by His grace; it is the aggregate multitude of those in heaven and on earth who love, adore, and serve the Son of God as their Redeemer and Lord. The very Greek word used in the New Testament for the Church helps define the Church, for *ekklesia* basically means "unity and calling," and it refers to the ordained unity Christ has offered and His separating out from the world those who will comprise His Church.

In speaking of the Church as the body of Christ, Paul alludes to a variety of principles.

As the body of Christ, the Church is one with Him. It is clearly stated, "He is the head of the body. . . ." Greater unity cannot be found. Recently in a convention where I was a participant, David du Plessis remarked, "On my passport they only have a picture of my head. The body is expected and accepted but unimportant enough to put on the passport." Where the headship of Jesus is seen, it is expected that there will be a body that functions in perfect unity with Him, for it shares a common source of life, and all activities of the body are governed by the head. Jesus taught that whatever is done to a member of the body is accepted as though done directly to the head: "Inasmuch as ye have done it unto one of the least of these my brethren, ye have done it unto me" (Matthew 25:40), so great is our oneness to Him.

Furthermore, *as the body of Christ, the Church has many cooperating and mutually dependent members.* There are varieties of offices, giftings, abilities, and ministries, but there is an interrelationship that brings unity. In calling us the body of Christ, Paul established that we are not an organization but an organism. We are animated, not actuated; it is a common life source that brought us into being, that unites us, and that motivates our actions. Because we are a body we are completive, not competitive. Paul underscored this conclusively in 1 Corinthians 12:14–20 by reminding us that "the body is not one member but many," and then pointing out how important it is for each member to function harmoniously with other members. In the natural, when a portion of our body does something, every other portion automatically supports it. It doesn't need a vote, require a conscious signal from the head, or even require a committee session; it just does it. Should not the spiritual body be equally united and animated by the common life of our Lord Jesus Christ? Happy is the Church whose members know their place and function in the duties distributed by the Spirit of God without coveting another's giftings or ministry.

Additionally, *as the body of Christ the Church is growing up to completeness and maturity.* We are not created complete; we are born as babes in Christ and must mature to the measure of the stature of a man in Christ Jesus. It is not intended that the Church be a perpetual nursery, for its members should "grow up into him in all things, which is the head, even Christ" (Ephesians 4:15). The reason Jesus does not translate new converts immediately is that time is needed to perfect the elect, bringing us into conformity to the image of God, which will be our eternal inheritance. Any who have visited a hospital and viewed a fully developed and matured head on a child's body know how frustrating a sight the Church will be if she refuses to continue to mature, develop, and grow to match the exceeding greatness of her Head; but Christ, our Head, is directing our development.

Moreover, *as the body of Christ, the Church is being restored to perfect soundness and health.* When Christ receives the new members to His body/Church they are "dead in trespasses and sins" (Ephesians 2:1); it is almost akin to transplanting a dead heart into a living body. The first thing that Jesus does is give us life and teach us to "likewise reckon ye also yourselves to be dead indeed unto sin, but alive unto God through Jesus Christ our Lord" (Romans 6:11). Even after the initial quickening, each believer needs subsequent life and healing in order to continue to function properly in the body, for just as our natural body is in a constant state of being torn down and rebuilt, so Christ's body suffers wounds, sickness, and invading disease, and needs a life force working within that is greater than the invading forces without. Jesus, the Great Physician, keeps His body in soundness and health when He is obeyed.

Similarly, *as the body of Christ, the Church is the object of His unremitting care.* Jesus has made ample provision for all the needs in His body. There is more than a sufficiency of graces, giftings, officers, anointings, blessings, and enablings to fulfill every legitimate desire any member could have. The Psalmist declared, ". . . the Lord will give grace and glory: no good thing will he withhold from them that walk uprightly" (Psalms 84:11). History is filled with the testimony of thousands of believers who have found that "my God shall supply all your need according to his riches in glory by Christ Jesus" (Philippians 4:19). Recession, inflation, war, drought, famine, pestilence, or strife do not deter our Lord Jesus from making ample provision for His body, the Church, for "God is able to make all grace abound toward you; that ye, always having all sufficiency in all things, may abound to every good work" (2 Corinthians 9:8). In the simple language of the shepherd, "The Lord is my shepherd; I shall not want" (Psalms 23:1).

Also, *as the body of Christ, the Church is the instrument through which He accomplishes His purposes.* In speaking of Jesus the Scripture says, "Sacrifice and offering thou wouldest not, but a body hast thou prepared me" (Hebrews 10:5). The work of God could not be accomplished merely in the offering of animal sacrifices; it required a body to satisfy God's needs. Actually Jesus required three bodies in order to fulfill the desires and needs of God the Father. First, He needed a body that could die, and God provided that through Mary. The Atonement was predicated upon death, and this body went to the cross in the place of sinful men and died the death we deserved. Second, Jesus needed a body that could ascend and live in the heavens. At the Resurrection God provided a glorified body for His Son, one that will never again taste of death, and one that is the prototype of the body that will be ours through eternity. Third, God gave Jesus a body that could function on this earth— the Church. The body of Jesus is wherever He has believers. The reason for a functioning body is to get the job done where the need is, and the body of Christ is alive and functioning right here on planet earth. All of the unbelief of sinful men and proud religious practitioners is not stopping the work of Jesus. His body will function, because God made it to function; and Jesus is the ordained Head of this body. As long as we own no other head, as long as we obey the orders of this Head, and as long as we rightly relate to the other members of this body, the world will not be without the ministry of the body of Christ Jesus.

There can be no question that the Church is the body of Jesus. Just as the head of the human body is one with the body, so Christ is corporately one in life and destiny with His redeemed saints, for at conversion the Holy Spirit baptizes the believers into the body of Christ (1 Corinthians 12:13) and at the same time into Christ the Head (Romans 6:3, 4). As the Head, Christ directs and controls all the activities of this body, which is also called His Church.

Jesus Is the Head of the Church

Thirteen times in the New Testament the word *church* is used for the universal body of believers, and ninety times it is used in reference to local assemblies. Jesus spoke of building the Church upon the foundation of Himself as the Christ when He told Peter, ". . . upon this rock I will build my church; and the gates of hell shall not prevail against it" (Matthew 16:18). Paul spoke of it as the body of Christ, and Peter revealed it as a "spiritual house" (1 Peter 2:5), while John the revelator saw Jesus standing in the midst of the churches (Revelation 1:13), but however it may be pictured and described, Jesus Christ is always the central figure. He is seen as its Foundation, its Head, its Capstone, and its Source of life.

In the Book to the Ephesians, Paul emphasizes the Church as the body of Christ, but here in Colossians he lays greater stress upon the headship of Christ over the Church: "He is the head of the body, the church. . . ." By the addition of the words *the Church*, it is impossible to consider the world as Christ's body. It has already been established that He is the authoritative Power over the entire universe, but here Paul speaks of an intimate relationship: Head of the body; Head of the Church. As the Head of the Church, Jesus inspires it with spiritual life and activity; He impresses and molds its character; He prescribes and enforces its laws; He governs and controls its destinies; He is the center of its unity. His glory and grace are so great that He can sustain life in the whole Church as well as rule and guide each member of it. Since He is the Head, our life is bound up with His life, and our interests are made His interests. We do not merely take orders; we partake of His life. We more than obey instructions; we interact and communicate with the One who is Head of the Church.

Books have been written about the Church, its calling, its government, its officers, and so on, but our limited space here allows only a brief discussion of Jesus as the Head of the Church. He is the Founder and Builder of His Church. It is His Church! He who is "the image of the invisible God, and the firstborn of every creature" (Colossians 1:15) is equally the Head, the Source of life, and the nerve center of His Church. Just as from our brain comes the direction for the movements of our body, so from Christ the movements of the Church are originated, guided, combined, and controlled, and as the brain with its connecting network of nerves can be present in all the body, so Christ is present in all the members of the Church.

As the Head of this mystical Church, He is the one and only absolute Authority within that Church. Offices and officers have been designated in the Church, but the Lord has never delegated His authority to any of them. Christ needs no vicar in His Church, because He is not absent from her; He is her Head, a vital, living, functioning part of the Church of God. The Church is not a company of people gathered around the memory of a dead and lost leader; it is constituted by the abiding presence of Jesus Himself, for He declared, "Where two or three are gathered together in my name, there am I in the midst of them" (Matthew 18:20). Jesus abides forevermore in the midst of His Church, and His will must be the final authority within His Church concerning every individual member, and concerning every detail of the manifold and complex life of every individual member and, consequently, concerning the whole Church as to the methods of its service, as to the meaning of its service, and as to the processes by which it fulfills that service. He, Jesus, is the government of the Church: He is the head over all things to the Church.

Few would disagree with this premise, but the immediate question that arises is, "How is this authority of our Lord to be applied in the actual corporate life of the Christian Church?" It is important to remind ourselves that although Christ Jesus gave us some teaching about the Church, He strongly insisted that the early apostles of that Church do nothing to bring it into existence until they had been endued with the Spirit of God on the day of Pentecost. Having instructed them for about three years, and having demonstrated His divinity in His Resurrection, He gave them the great Gospel commission and then cautioned them, "Behold, I send the promise of my Father upon you: but tarry ye in the city of Jerusalem, until ye be endued with power from on high" (Luke 24:49), and just before His Ascension He promised them, "But ye shall receive power, after that the Holy Ghost is come upon you: and ye shall be witnesses unto me . . ." (Acts 1:8). The Church was not birthed until the Spirit came on the day of Pentecost, for the Holy Spirit is Christ's representative in His body, the Church, just as Jesus was the Representative of the Father on the shores of Galilee. Jesus is present in the lives of His believers through the indwelling Spirit of God.

The Book of Acts, which records the rise of the Early Church with its persecutions, problems, and great victories, is a book of the continued works of Jesus. Luke begins his book by saying, "The former treatise have I made, O Theophilus, of all that Jesus began both to do and teach" (Acts 1:1), suggesting that the Gospel of Luke is completed in the Book of Acts, which is all that Jesus continued to do and teach, for although Jesus left this earth physically, the Holy Spirit returned to indwell individual believers and to direct the corporeal Church. Christ is not absent from His Church; therefore all attempts to substitute an authority within the Church for that of the living Christ are wrong. There is no need for mediation between the authority of Christ and His Church beyond the mediation of the Spirit, for the ministry of the Holy Spirit in interpreting the will of Jesus is immediate and direct, as the Book of Acts illustrates.

No amount of human organization has ever deposed Christ from His position as the Head of the Church. He will still speak to His Church, if she is prepared to listen. He will indicate His will, if His people are waiting to know that will. The Holy Spirit will perfectly equip Christ's people for the doing of His work in the world by the bestowment of gifts necessary for that work. The indwelling Spirit of God still knows what is the mind of Christ and has been commissioned to share that with us. The Church should be in direct contact with this supreme will, for none but Christ Jesus dare direct the Church of the living God.

Is it not possible that some of the reasons for the ineptness, anemia, weakness, and outright failure of today's Church can be traced to the fact that we have been trying to govern the Church by our own wit and wisdom seeking to find a way to do God's work instead of remembering that the living Lord is at the center of the Christian Church, and that the living Spirit, and not past interpretations, constitutes the method of guidance and direction in all our work?

For the past few years in America, there has been much preaching about the need for unity in the Church. Understandably, the methods prescribed for attaining that unity have been as varied as the backgrounds of the speakers. Some have sought unity in doctrine, others in experience, and still others in an authoritarian control of people's lives, but the body will be gloriously unified when it again recognizes Christ Jesus as the Head of the Church and learns how to communicate with that Head in prayer and supplication. Our disunity is alarming evidence that all are not hearing from the same head. Our problems are not structural, organizational, doctrinal, or conceptual; the government of the Lord Jesus Christ within His own Church is principally interfered with when we are not in right relationship with the Paraclete, the Advocate, the Comforter, the Holy Spirit Himself.

Jesus Is the Firstborn From the Dead

Paul continues to magnify the Lord Jesus by titling Him "the beginning, the firstborn from the dead" (Colossians 1:18). That He is the Beginning of all things that exist has already been established. Here it is merely reaffirmed that Jesus is the beginning of the Church also. Jesus is the originating, fontal Source of the organic life of the Church. He gives to the Church its existence, form, history, and glory; and the Church could have no existence except in and through Him.

He who was the Author of the old material creation is here called the Author of the moral creation. He is the beginning of the new spiritual creation which forms the basis for and the elements of the Church. In the development of this new creation, Jesus will undo all the havoc and ruin occasioned by the wrongdoing of the old creation. The old life will pass away and the new life will come (2 Corinthians 5:17). All that was lost in Adam will be restored in Christ in His Church. He is both "Alpha and Omega, the beginning and the ending" (Revelation 1:8). Anything Jesus begins He completes, and He began a Church and has promised to "present it to himself a glorious church, not having spot, or wrinkle, or any such thing; but that it should be holy and without blemish" (Ephesians 5:27).

As the Author of the moral creation He also is the Conqueror of death: "the firstborn from the dead." It was sin that introduced death into the old creation, and Jesus came to put away sin, even tasting death Himself, descending into Hades and placing Himself among the dead. But on the third day He rose again as "the firstfruits of them that slept" (1 Corinthians 15:20).

In calling Jesus "the firstborn from the dead," the Scripture is not declaring Him the first to come forth from the grave, for resurrections happened even in Old Testament times, but all who were raised to life eventually had to die again. Jesus not only died voluntarily but He also rose by His own power (John 2:19), never to die again (Romans 6:9), and was clothed in an immortal body (Revelation 1:18). He, the Head of the Church, by also becoming the "firstborn from the dead," has become the cause, pledge, and pattern of our resurrection. As the "firstfruits" were an indication and pledge of the harvest, so surely was the Resurrection of Christ the proof that all mankind should have a resurrection from the dead.

But the expression "the firstborn from the dead" is not a full translation of the Greek word Paul used, for it is difficult to get a word to express the whole meaning. One writer suggests this idea: that Christ Jesus exists in that in which He operated. He is the great Energizer incarnate. When He rose from the dead He was not only the possessor of a new life Himself but He is also regenerative cause to those who come after Him. "He is our life" (*see* Colossians 3:4) who said, "because I live, ye shall live also" (John 14:19).

As the Head of the Church and the "firstborn from the dead" Jesus Christ not only assures the beginning of the Church but also its final ending in heaven with the saints of the ages who await our coming, for "he which hath begun a good work in you will perform it until the day of Jesus Christ" (Philippians 1:6).

Jesus Has the Preeminence

The declared purpose of placing Jesus as the Head of the body and Head of the Church, and further declaring Him the beginning and "the firstborn from the dead" is "that in all things he might have the preeminence" (Colossians 1:18). This is merely a further unfolding of truth already stated, for we have seen that Jesus is preeminent in His relation to the Father, because He is "the image of the invisible God" (verse 15). He is preeminent in the universe of created beings, for He is "the firstborn of every creature" (verse 15). He is preeminent in His rule over the realm of the dead, for He is "the firstborn from the dead" (verse 18). Furthermore, He is preeminent in His relation to the Church, for "he is the head of the body, the church" (verse 18). Now Paul adds that He is preeminent in the estimation and homage of a ransomed world, for "in all things he might have the preeminence" (verse 18). Jesus is the central figure in all things past, present, and future.

Paul stresses the cardinal point in the Christology of the New

Testament: the existence of one mediator presiding over the two spheres—the universe and the Church. Some have mistakenly or confusedly purported that it is God in nature and Christ in the Church, but it is really Christ in both. He mediated in Creation before He mediated in Redemption. This absolute preeminence of Christ implies a unity of meaning and a harmony of working between these two spheres. Since Jesus Christ is preeminent in the universe, everywhere we go we are surrounded by His acts, His laws, His control, and His love. Whether in temple or forest, His presence is equally available. Since Jesus is preeminent in the Church, we know that all things can be placed at the service of the Church—things natural and things spiritual. Worldly powers are controlled for the Church. The day is coming when commerce, science, art, literature, and finance shall all be consecrated to Him, when the minority shall become a majority, and an innumerable multitude shall "honour the Son, even as they honour the Father . . ." (John 5:23).

This preeminence of Jesus Christ is assured by "the fulness" that abides in Him. "For it pleased the Father that in him should all fulness dwell" (Colossians 1:19). God has placed in Jesus the complete fullness and exhaustless perfection of the divine essence, the theologians tell us. We may more simply take the term in its widest signification—a fullness of life and power and glory, of goodness and grace, without limit and without end, and because all the majesty, power, and goodness of God is manifested in and by Christ Jesus, the Father through Him has reconciled all things to Himself.

13

Jesus, the Reconcilor

". . . by him to reconcile all things unto himself. . . . And you . . . now hath he reconciled" (Colossians 1:20,21).

After declaring that God was pleased to have all of His fullness dwell in Jesus (1:19) Paul doesn't even break his sentence but continues by saying, "And, having made peace through the blood of his cross, by him to reconcile all things unto himself . . . whether they be things in earth, or things in heaven" (Colossians 1:20), thereby reminding us that it is only through the propitiatory sacrifice of Jesus as God's spotless Lamb that peace between God and man could be effected. Sin keeps man set on a course of confrontation with God; it is open hostility to God, for sin is both a violation of God's will and word and an active involvement with our own way (Isaiah 53:6). There is no hope of friendly relationships between men and God until the sin issue has been settled, and ". . . the blood of Jesus Christ . . . cleanseth us from all sin" (1 John 1:7). Redemption must always precede reconciliation, but it does not necessarily or automatically produce it, for reconciliation is a separate and subsequent act in the life of the believer.

When Hezekiah reinstated Temple worship after the death of his father, Ahaz, who had locked the gates of the Temple, he very deliberately separated the sin offerings from the offerings for reconciliation. After the bullocks, rams, and lambs had been offered for the sins of the people nationally and individually, Hezekiah instructed the priests to offer seven he goats, "and they made reconciliation with their blood upon the altar . . ." (2 Chronicles 29:24).

The purpose of the sacrificing of these goats was to bring the king, princes, priests, and people back into a friendly relationship with God.

Paul maintains this same order in the New Testament theology of reconciliation. First sin is settled and then the separation between man and God is bridged. Propitiation, peace, and reconciliation are always the divine order. Speaking both of the great distance and alienation between the Gentiles and the Jews and the Gentiles and God, Paul wrote, "But now in Christ Jesus ye who sometimes were far off are made nigh by the blood of Christ. For he is our peace ... that he might reconcile both unto God ..." (Ephesians 2:13,14,16). Sin cleansed, peace certified, and believers conciliated are progressive works of the cross, each dependent upon the former.

The Greek word Paul employs here for "reconcile" is *katallassō,* which means "to change, or exchange." It was the word used to describe the action of the Temple moneychangers who exchanged the foreign currency of the worshipers for the Temple shekel. It would be the word used to describe the action of today's travelers who go to a bank to exchange U.S. dollars for German marks, Japanese yen, or Argentine pesos. But when the word is used of persons it always means to change from enmity to friendship.

Therefore, Paul is declaring that Jesus Christ is actively engaged in making it possible for us to exchange our hatred for His love, our withdrawal from Him for His nearness to us. We are invited to step out of our enmity against God into a friendship with God.

In saying that Jesus chose to "reconcile all things unto himself ... whether they be things in earth, or things in heaven" (Colossians 1:20), Paul painted an opaque picture that has become almost a labyrinth for interpreters. Some scholars feel that the "all things" refers to "by him were all things created, that are in heaven, and that are in earth ..." (verse 16), thereby insisting that Jesus must and will bring everything that exists back into a harmonious relationship with Himself, even the devil and his kingdom. The most common title for their doctrine is "The Ultimate Reconciliation of All Things," and it has been revived in the past twenty or so years. Its zealous proponents often have great difficulty explaining the teachings of Jesus on hell and the prophecies of the final book of the Bible.

Other teachers, often very gifted in the Greek language of the New Testament, insist that the "all things" must be confined to "the blood of his cross," limiting reconciliation to that which has been redeemed, making the reference to the "heavens" mean the Old Testament saints who have already gone to Paradise, who were under a provisional atonement but now are reconciled by the actual shedding of Christ's blood, and the "earth" to mean the New Testament saints who have lived since Calvary.

Adam Clarke, a gifted expositor, offers a third view by suggesting that Paul speaks here of the contrast between the relationship of the Jews and the Gentiles to Christ, alluding to the state of the covenant Jews as being divine or celestial while the state of the Gentiles was considered merely earthly.

Obviously this subject has been discussed and speculated on since the day Paul wrote in such generalities, but its mystery remains hidden with Christ in God. We do know that sin is an alien force that was introduced to earth from outside, and that it is responsible both for the separation of man from God and for the chaos of the whole creation. Heaven was the point of origin for sin, and it had to be purified by the blood of Jesus (Hebrews 9:23). Whatever else must be done to restore divine things to their pristine state is beyond the imaginations of men, but it is wholly within the scope of God's plan of restoration.

From these speculative generalities Paul moves immediately to the specific and personal in saying, "And you . . . hath he reconciled" (verse 21). This we can look at with full assurance of faith, for regardless of what or who Jesus chooses to reconcile in His great creation, He has specifically promised and provided to reconcile the believing saint!

The Need for Reconciliation

While it may be argued that Paul was specifically speaking to Gentiles and was illustrating how far they were from the covenant promises of God, it is equally true that all men are alienated from

God, and all are enemies in their minds to Him, showing it by their wicked works. Furthermore, Paul's use of the expression "that were sometime" (verse 21) can be applied to our pre-Calvary experience or to post-Calvary living. We have all met Christians who were alienated from God, who were not on speaking terms with God. Actually, many Christians harbor an anger or resentment against God, holding Him responsible for some real or imagined evil that had befallen them. They would not forsake following the Lord, for they fear Him, but they do forsake fellowshipping with the Lord. They have stopped shooting in their feud, but they have not started speaking to God. They need to be reconciled to God; they need to be changed from enmity to friendship.

The first reason we need to be reconciled, Paul says, is that we were alienated from God. "And you, that were sometime alienated ..." (verse 21). The Greek word which we here render *alienated* means "to give to another, to estrange," but by coupling it with the preposition *from*, it means "to estrange utterly, to be wholly the property of another." It implies a fixed condition that has become a part of man's nature. The word is used only one other time in the New Testament where it is translated, "alienated from the life of God" (Ephesians 4:18).

In turning to *Webster's Dictionary* to find out the shades of meaning of the English word we read, "To estrange; make unfriendly: to cause a transference of (affection)." It is in this third category that we best understand the word, for it has not been too unusual in American courts of law to have a suit filed against a person for "alienation of affections." The particulars in the suit may declare that the plaintiff once had the love, affection, respect, and connubial bliss of the man named, but this third party, who is being sued, "alienated his affections," thereby stealing his love and taking him out of the home.

It seems that Paul is suggesting that someone or something can steal our affection for Jesus Christ, thereby alienating us from Him. This was the charge against the Church in Ephesus: "Nevertheless I have somewhat against thee, because thou hast left thy first love" (Revelation 2:4).

As any believer can testify, after the initial exuberance of our newfound love for Jesus has lost its height of excitement, life, lust, vainglory, and a hundred other things, all endeavor to alienate our affections from Jesus to self. Whereas in the beginning Jesus was central in our love and thoughts, we are tempted, sometimes too easily, to once again become the center of our own affections and concerns. Almost any church group could give you the name of one or more individuals who were lifted from a life of sin into the glorious salvation of Jesus Christ, only to later become enamored with something of the old life, and progressively they were enticed away from Christ. They ended up totally alienated from Jesus.

In either case, the worship of the Lord Jesus Christ ceases, for none can truly worship when his affections yearn for another, since worship is fundamentally love responding to love. Any persons having an illicit affair outside their marriages can testify to their inability to respond positively to the love advances of their true mate, for their affections have been alienated and replaced with guilt feelings. So it is when we allow anything to become the object of our affections that had once been pledged to Jesus Christ.

We need to get a hold on our affections and control them, rather than allowing them to control us. Man was not created to be ruled by his soul, but by his spirit. Christians shouldn't even speak of "falling in love" as though some sinister force had tripped them into a helpless response. We *rise* to love, for love is a commitment and an act of our will. "God commendeth His love toward us . . ." (Romans 5:8), and similarly we are urged to "Set your affection on things above, not on things on the earth" (Colossians 3:2). Our affections follow the direction of our will. We do not serve the Lord out of an emotional response, but out of a devotional commitment, just as we do not declare ourselves married when the emotional surge of pleasure is flowing between the partners, and unmarried during discussions about the budget. The emotions rise and fall, but the commitment remains, unless we have allowed ourselves to become alienated from our partner by giving our love to another. When that happens, the Bible calls for reconciliation, while our culture calls for a divorce. Jesus does not want any form of separation from a saint; He wants us to be reconciled back to friendly fellowship.

Paul says that a second reason we need reconciliation is that we "were sometime . . . enemies in your mind . . ." (Colossians 1:21). Three other times the New Testament calls us enemies: "For if, when we were enemies, we were reconciled to God . . ."; ". . . know ye not that the friendship of the world is enmity with God? whosoever therefore will be a friend of the world is the enemy of God"; and, "The carnal mind is enmity against God . . ." (Romans 5:10; James 4:4; Romans 8:7).

It does not declare that God became our enemy, but that we mentally put ourselves into a state of warfare with God. It may be because His will violates our will, or His ways seem unpleasant and unbearable, or because we imagine that He has been unjust in His dealings in our lives. But whatever the reason, if we mentally consider ourselves at war with God, we obviously lose the peace of God and withdraw ourselves from the presence of God. While true love and righteous indignation can coexist, love and enmity cannot exist together. We cannot war against and worship God, so the war mentality must be replaced with a reconciled attitude. How carefully we need to approach our relationship with the world and the carnal life, for if we establish friendly relations there, we automatically lose our friendly relations with God. It is but another form of alienation.

Still a third reason we need reconciliation is "wicked works" (Colossians 1:21). This may not mean that the Christian is involved in doing wicked works, but that he is so vexed with the wickedness around him that he loses his love relationship with Jesus. It is written of Lot that he was "vexed with the filthy conversation of the wicked" (2 Peter 2:7). The manner of life, mores, morals, and wickedness of sinful men and women can affect our attitudes and actions. Even watching such wickedness on television can affect our attitude toward God and His Word. Those who work with the ungodly cannot help being affected by their speech, stories, swearing, and sinfulness, for it wears upon them like the dropping of water, or the blowing of sand in the wind.

In Peter's Second Epistle he warns, "Beware lest ye also, being led away with the error of the wicked, fall from your own steadfastness" (2 Peter 3:17). In the preceding verse he wrote about "some things hard to be understood, which they that are un-learned and unstable wrest, as they do also the other scriptures, unto their own destruction" (verse 16). How plagued religion has been with this form of wickedness—twisting Scripture to fit pet doctrines. This will cost us the joy of a relationship with God, and once we gullibly swallow teaching that purports to be God's Word but is actually a perversion of it, we become prime candidates for reconciliation, for none need it more than we. False concepts produce false conclusions about God and His ways and always end up separating us from God rather than bringing us to God, because God is not what we *think* He is but who He *says* He is, and He warns us:

> For my thoughts are not your thoughts, neither are your ways my ways, saith the Lord. For as the heavens are higher than the earth, so are my ways higher than your ways, and my thoughts than your thoughts.
>
> Isaiah 55:8,9

So Paul suggests that our tendency to become alienated, coupled with an inherent predisposition to be enemies of God in our minds (if nothing more than the exercise of the self-will in opposition to the divine will), and our reactions to or reception of wicked works, all create a need for fresh reconciliation with God. It is always man's tendency to "turn unto his own way" (*see* Isaiah 53:6) that creates the need for a new start in fellowshipping with God. Never once does the New Testament speak of God's needing to be reconciled with man, for God is never pictured as being at enmity with man. Although Israel was said to be "estranged from God" (*see* Ezekiel 14:5), God constantly manifested His love toward her. Reconciliation, then, is not propitiating the anger of God but settling the anger of man. It does not, strictly speaking, bring God to man; it brings man to God.

The Basis of Reconciliation

After telling us that God commended His love toward us even while we were still sinners, and that He has justified us by the blood of Jesus, Paul assures us, "If, when we were enemies, we were reconciled to God by the death of his Son, much more, being reconciled, we shall be saved by his life" (Romans 5:10). There is no other basis for reconciliation with God than the vicarious, substitutionary, atoning death of Jesus on the cross. The animal sacrifices of the Old Testament merely looked forward to the true sacrifice of God's Lamb—Jesus Christ. Since it is sin that alienated us from God, and the cross is God's only answer to sin, our reconciliation to God is integrally tied to the Atonement. Christ's death both put away sin and restored fellowship with the Godhead, for we identify not only with Christ's death but also with His life of fellowship with the Father.

We do well to remember that sin did not catch God napping or change His mind in any way. Satan's sneak attack in Eden caught God neither off guard nor unprepared. God had purposed, provided, and planned to redeem man by Christ's death even before the foundations of the world were originally laid (1 Peter 1:20). God did not have plan *A* for a sinless race and plan *B* for a sinning race; God had *a plan,* and that plan was the death of Jesus at Calvary. In a marvelous way that exceeds our comprehension, even sin is part of God's process to bring us fully into the image of God, and this plan is traced back to the beginning of Creation, for Paul declares:

Blessed be the God and Father of our Lord Jesus Christ, who hath blessed us with all spiritual blessings in heavenly places in Christ: According as he hath chosen us in him before the foundation of the world, that we should be holy and without blame before him in love.

Ephesians 1:3,4

That the only basis of our reconciliation is the work of Jesus is beautifully underscored by the Spirit in Paul's inspired words, ". . . but we also rejoice in God through our Lord Jesus Christ, through whom we have now received reconciliation" (Romans 5:11 NIV). God purposed reconciliation for man, Jesus purchased it, and the Holy Spirit positions man "in heavenly places in Christ Jesus" (Ephesians 2:6), so that:

he might reconcile both [Jews and Gentiles] unto God in one body by the cross, having slain the enmity thereby. . . . For through him we both have access by one Spirit unto the Father . . . ye also are builded together for an habitation of God through the Spirit.

Ephesians 2:16,18,22

The Nature of Reconciliation

In his Second Letter to the Corinthians, Paul speaks of reconciliation as:

Therefore, if anyone is in Christ, he is a new creation; the old has gone, the new has come! All this is from God, who reconciled us to himself through Christ and gave us the ministry of reconciliation: that God was reconciling the world to himself in Christ, not counting men's sins against them. And he has committed to us the message of reconciliation.

2 Corinthians 5:17–19 NIV

Reconciliation is fundamentally a changed condition in man so that all basis of the enmity relationship is removed and a new basis of approach to God is established. It is a change from a sin-based approach to a grace-based approach. The old relationship went when God removed the old nature, and the new basis of approach came with the new nature.

It may be poetically beautiful to sing, "Only a sinner, saved by grace," but it is without scriptural foundation, for once a person appropriates to himself God's provision of Christ's death, the New Testament never refers to him as a sinner. He is called a saint, a son, a bride, and an heir of God, but never a sinner; for although he is actually a saint in the making, a son maturing, a bride in preparation, and an heir in waiting, he is never seen as a sinner in the process of being saved, although we all realize that there is a marvelous progressive side to our salvation.

Lacking this understanding, the Christian may try to approach God on a sin basis, reconfessing old sins, claiming to be nothing but sinful flesh full of carnal mistakes. This attitude will prevent fellowship with God, for no sinner dare approach the presence of a holy God. Conversely, when we recognize our conferred standing before God because of the work of Jesus Christ, we come into His presence as sons, not sinners.

When my three daughters still lived at home I gave them keys to our house, car, church, and my office. I instructed them that if they wanted to see me when I was at the church they neither needed an appointment nor the permission of my secretary to enter my study. "Just use your key and come right in," I told them. I wanted them to know that they had rights as my daughters that no member of my congregation would ever have. They were bone of my bone and flesh of my flesh, and I wanted them to approach me as my children, not as part of the congregation. And, of course, they delighted in checking this out.

Because of our changed nature, we now have a change in our relationship to God. By the process of the new birth we have become "sons of God," "children of God," and are even declared "members of his body, of his flesh, and of his bones" (Ephesians 5:30). This radically affects the basis of our approach to God. We are part of the "family of God" who have been invited to share fellowship with the Father. Our changed *condition* (Calvary) produced changed *relationships* ("Now are we the sons of God") which fosters a change of *attitude* and *affection* toward God.

> Therefore, brothers, since we have confidence to enter the Most Holy Place by the blood of Jesus, by a new and living way opened for us through the curtain, that is, his body, and since we have a great priest over the house of God, let us draw near to God with a sincere heart in full assurance of faith, having our hearts sprinkled to cleanse us from a guilty conscience and having our bodies washed with pure water.
>
> Hebrews 10:19–22 NIV

Although the imputing of righteousness to men removes all barriers to fellowship with God and establishes a totally new basis for fellowshipping with Him, man is not automatically reconciled by accepting the death of Jesus as efficacious for his sins; there must be a change of mind and concepts about God and a subsequent change in his attitudes and affections. The cross totally satisfied

God; it is man who must now be totally satisfied in the cross. Since God did not withdraw from man it becomes man's responsibility to initiate the return to God. Man must discipline himself to release the old and to embrace the new if he is to enjoy a reconciled relationship with God.

The Purpose of Reconciliation

While the obvious purpose of reconciliation is a restored relationship to God similar to that which Adam enjoyed in Eden, Paul tells the Colossians that there are three additional purposes, all of which flow together and make this intimate fellowship possible. "And you ... hath he reconciled ... to present you *holy* and *unblameable* and *unreproveable* in his sight" (Colossians 1:21,22, italics added), he writes.

"Reconciled ... to present you *holy* ... his sight." What a contrast to the way we appear in our sight, yet this is the way Jesus intends to present His beloved to Himself in the heavenlies. Accomplishing this feat is dependent upon Jesus, not the individual believers, for we are totally powerless to produce holy natures. Paul had spoken of this goal of Christ in his letter to the Ephesians when he wrote:

> Christ loved the Church and gave himself up for her to make her holy, cleansing her by the washing with water through the word, and to present her to himself as a radiant church, without stain or wrinkle or any other blemish, but holy and blameless.
>
> Ephesians 5:25–27 NIV

Since holiness is the prime essential of the divine nature of Christ, we are offered an opportunity to share in that very nature, for the more we are like Him the easier and the more profitable fellowship with Him will be. He has provided all things needful to make us holy; we need but appropriate and apply them, and even in that responsibility the Holy Spirit resides to help us.

"Reconciled ... to present you *unblameable* ... in his sight," is given as an additional purpose of our reconciliation to God. Oh, how the "accuser of the brethren" (*see* Revelation 12:10) loves to heap blame upon the children of God. He projects guilt for every failure of human flesh, and seeks to convince us that we have forfeited our right of access to God for the smallest infraction of the rules, and he has plenty of help from our own accusing heart. Howbeit, in reconciling us to a family relationship with God, all the blame for our misdeeds goes to Jesus, not us, for the parent is responsible for the behavior of the children.

When my girls were small they loved to play on the lawn in the backyard of our neighbor. One day I saw my girls and the neighbor's girl playing softball with the catcher's back dangerously close to the large dining-room window. I quickly realigned the diamond for them and strongly prohibited any further playing of ball near that window. Sometime later I was in my home study when the back door to our house burst open and three excited girls tore upstairs to their bedroom, and then everything became quiet, until there came an agitated knock on my front door. Standing there was our neighbor with a piece of broken glass in one hand and a softball in the other. Instinctively I knew what had happened.

"What are you going to do about it?" is all that he said.

He didn't ask to see my girls; he offered no suggestion of punishment for them; he dealt entirely with me, for their actions were my legal responsibility. I replaced his window before the day was over, and then chastened my daughters for their disobedience.

Although my girls were guilty of breaking a window, they were unblameable to the neighbor; the blame was mine. So our Heavenly Father accepts the blame for our misbehavior. He does not turn us over to the devil or even to godless men to face the blame; He faces it for us and then chastens us back into obedience.

Finally, Paul says you have been "Reconciled . . . to present you *unreproveable* in his sight." In the Ephesian letter Paul uses a similar list of three, but there he speaks of our being "before him in love" rather than "unreproveable" (Ephesians 1:4). When the eyes of the beholder are filled with love, there is little seen that needs reproof. God always sees us through His love. He is not a stern jurist seeking to enforce every subsection of His law; He is a loving Father enjoying having His children around Him. It was He who established the principle that "Love is the fulfilling of the Law" (Romans

13:1), so when His children come into His presence with unmitigated love and complete abandonment in expressing that love, God sees the law as sufficiently fulfilled in our lives. Oh, this does not rule out further training and new guidelines for behavior, but it does mean we can come into His presence without being reproved by Him. His love for us and our love for Him combine to make us "unreproveable in His sight."

Jesus, the Source of our grace, peace, love, and hope, who has become the Object of our faith, our Deliverer, our King, our Redeemer, the very image of God, the preexistent Creator who sustains all things; Jesus, the Head of the body and the Church, the beginning, the firstborn from the dead, the preeminent One in whom all the fullness of the Father dwells, is also our Reconcilor whose goal is to return us to the innocence our first parents had in the presence of the Father. He would have us be comfortable in God's presence and conformed to the divine image. He has chosen to share His works, His power, His authority, His position, and His very nature with us, for He has made us "Children, then heirs; heirs of God, and joint-heirs with Christ ..." (Romans 8:17). Everything He is and has is shared with us on an equal basis, for "joint-heir" does not signify fifty-fifty; it means each owns all. It is like a joint checking account; both have access to everything.

"... And who is sufficient for these things?" (2 Corinthians 2:16), we may ask. Jesus answers for us, "My grace is sufficient for thee: for my strength is made perfect in weakness ..." (2 Corinthians 12:9).